Deborah Witherspoon
3963 Brightgold LN
Canal Winchester
OHIO 43110
(614) 920-4759

CPR II

Tuesday - 9
Wednesday - 9
FRiday - 9

ON THE BRINK

OTHER BOOKS BY ROD PARSLEY

Daily Breakthrough

The Day Before Eternity

No Dry Season

No More Crumbs

ON THE BRINK

BREAKING THROUGH EVERY OBSTACLE

INTO THE GLORY OF GOD

ROD PARSLEY

Publishers Since 1798

THOMAS NELSON PUBLISHERS®
Nashville

Published in Nashville, Tennessee, by Thomas Nelson, Inc.

Unless otherwise noted, the Scripture quotations are from THE KING JAMES VERSION of the Bible.

Scripture quotations noted AMPLIFIED are from THE AMPLIFIED BIBLE: Old Testament. Copyright © 1962, 1964 by Zondervan Publishing House (used by permission); and from THE AMPLI-FIED NEW TESTAMENT. Copyright © 1958 by the Lockman Foundation (used by permission).

Library of Congress Cataloging-in-Publication Data

Parsley, Rod
    On the brink : breaking through every obstacle into the glory of God / Rod Parsley.
       p. cm.
    Includes bibliographical references.
    ISBN 0-7852-6808-1
    1. Christian Life—United States. I. Title.
    BV4501 .2 .P352365 2000
    243—dc21

                        00-042365
                            CIP

Printed in the United States of America

2 3 4 5 6 BVG 05 04 03 02 01 00

CONTENTS

CHAPTER 1

LIVING ON THE BRINK

The preacher's son was born in a time of big cities and high-rise structures. Everyone believed it was "the best of times" because business had never been better. The moguls of the financial world were working seven days a week cutting deals and making money at levels beyond their wildest dreams. New advances in the sciences and the arts were revolutionizing the way people viewed their world and expressed themselves. Things were so good that entertainment and pleasure became the driving forces behind the society.

The problem was that the "best" wasn't the best after all. A gloom was pressing down over the surface-level frivolity, as if all of the laughter and drunkenness was nothing more than a nervous attempt to hide or cover up a bone-deep fear of what tomorrow would bring.

The preacher's son was in a tough place. How could he refuse all of the pleasures that paraded before his eyes day after day so that he could follow in his forefathers' footsteps? The pressure to conform was almost irresistible, and support for his father's values didn't exist. He felt like a stranger, like a pilgrim living in a foreign land.

Most of the people around the preacher's son were like his distant cousin. Both of them were seventh in line from the same great-, great-, great-, great-grandfather. The cousin of the preacher's son was a powerful man who openly bragged that he had killed a man for wounding him, and that he had even killed a boy who dared to hit him.

He was a "champion" for individual rights and personal freedom of expression at any cost. The story played well in the city, especially when he bragged that anyone who dared to bring him to justice would be cursed 490 times with an ancient curse of power descended from his ancestor. He was also a polygamist with three sons famed for their abilities in the commodities market, the music industry, and the visual arts, respectively. He was the epitome of the age: brash, fierce, rebellious, totally self-centered, and oblivious to any concept of right and wrong that didn't suit his individual will.

LIFE IS EASY AS LONG AS YOU FIT IN

For sixty-five years, the preacher's son lived without a testimony to set him apart from his cousin, or anyone else for that matter. Life was easy as long as he fit in, but somehow it didn't seem that he was really living. His daddy was a preacher, his daddy before him was a preacher, and so was his daddy before him. Yet no matter how many preachers were in his heritage, the preacher's son somehow sensed that he couldn't get in on Daddy's coattails. There has to come a time of decision, and for this preacher's son, it seems to have been his sixty-fifth year.

Perhaps something happened to this man when his first son was born. No witnesses have come forward to say that he walked with a limp after that day, and no one has claimed that he walked around with his face shining like the noonday sun. All we know from history is that *from that point on* he had the testimony that "he walked with God."

For sixty-five years the preacher's son walked with God in word only, but after his son was born, he became a companion of God. The man was changed so radically that immediately he began to stand out from everyone else in his society. He was compelled to speak with prophetic force against the sin and debauchery in his generation.

He declared that judgment was coming to his lawless and technologically advanced society, and his zeal for the truth unleashed a whirlwind of criticism, bigotry, and hatred against him. It didn't stop him; it merely spurred him to preach even harder about the warning signs of impending doom. It didn't have to come—there was a way out called repentance. Yet either way, he knew his society was on the brink of something big, something ominous.

The people in this man's era were steeped in religious falsehood, preoccupied with the accumulation of material things, and filled with spiritual darkness. Until his life-changing encounter with God, his "religion" had shown no power to impact his society. Does that sound familiar? What is the identity of this mystery man of God?

HE WALKED WITH GOD IN A POLLUTED AND PROMISCUOUS GENERATION

His name was Enoch, and he was born only seven generations after Adam's creation by God (Adam was still alive when Enoch was born). He stood head and shoulders above the rest of the men in his generation, including the rest of the preachers in his family. How did he do it? What set Enoch apart from the crowd? *He walked with God in the middle of a polluted and promiscuous generation.*

Enoch knew judgment and destruction were coming. Evidently he and his wife were careful to raise their children in the fear and the admonition of the Lord because God chose his great-grandson to preserve the human race when judgment fell. His name was *Noah*.

The last mention of Enoch in the Bible appears in some verses of the book of Jude, just before the beginning of the book of Revelation. It is interesting that this man who walked with God shows up at the very beginning and at the very end of God's Word:

Enoch also, the seventh from Adam, *prophesied of these, saying, Behold, the Lord cometh with ten thousands of his saints, to execute judgment upon all,* and to convince all that are ungodly among them of all their ungodly deeds which they have ungodly committed, and of all their hard speeches which ungodly sinners have spoken against him. These are murmurers, complainers, walking after their own lusts; and their mouth speaketh great swelling words, having men's persons in admiration because of advantage. (Jude 14–16, italics mine)

ENOCH PROPHESIED THE LORD'S SECOND COMING

If we read through this scripture passage as we usually do, we may miss the obvious. Do you see what Enoch did? *He prophesied the Lord's second coming "with ten thousands of his saints."*[1]

Enoch peered through the telescope of prophecy beyond the impending Flood of Noah, all the way past the Old Testament patriarchs and the major and minor prophets of old, to witness the miraculous arrival of the Son of man in a lowly Bethlehem manger amid the lowing of the cattle.

In tears and dismay, he watched soldiers in unfamiliar armor and clothing nail God's Son to a cross where He hung suspended between heaven and earth. He watched Jesus' friends bury Him in a borrowed tomb, and he rejoiced to see the Lamb of God raised up on the third day and witnessed His ascent to the Father.

Enoch walked in the Spirit with a prophetic vision that pierced beyond the thin veil of time all the way to the apostolic age, the church age, and even through the age of grace in which we live. His Spirit-guided gaze saw past the "catching up" of the saints and the seven years of tribulation to witness the second coming of the King of glory "with ten thousands of his saints."

Enoch's society was much like ours. It was enmeshed in a tangle of self-gratification, hedonism (extreme pleasure seeking), murder, and satanic worship. It was the seedbed for an uncontrolled epidemic of pornography and deviant sexual practices.

Yet Enoch's story is more than a tale of sin and impending doom; it is also a story of God's great mercy and grace. Enoch somehow managed to have a testimony that few, if any, people have today, yet he lived and raised his children in the middle of a spiritual and social cesspool. His testimony is that he walked with God before there was a cross or a resurrection, yet he pleased Him and was obedient to warn his generation of coming judgment.

ENOCH'S LIFE WAS LIVING PROOF OF
GOD'S PRESENCE

Is that your testimony? Enoch's life was living proof of God's presence in the midst of a perverse age. The reward for Enoch's faithfulness is unmatched in the Bible with the possible exceptions of Elijah's ascension in a chariot of fire (2 Kings 2:11) and our Lord's ascension in the clouds (Acts 1:9). The Scriptures tell us, "[Enoch] was not; for God took him" (Gen. 5:24). God removed what was His before He cleaned house.

Before God took Enoch unto Himself, He commissioned him to prophesy "repentance or judgment" to his generation as God's wrath built up in the heavenlies. The God of grace and mercy waited for three more generations and sent yet another preacher and descendant of Enoch, Noah, to declare the truth before the end came.

Meanwhile, the Lord said to Himself, "Before I release one ounce of My wrath on this obstinate race, there is *one man who walks with Me* on the earth whom I refuse to lose. I need to get him out of there." As for the other people, they got to ride out the Flood.

It appears that any of them could have purchased a ticket on Noah's salvation cruise for the price of true repentance.

Noah was the only other man of that era known as a man who "walked with God," and it was his destiny to ride out the storm under the protection of God. Not Enoch. Enoch didn't know anything about storing up food, hoarding money, transferring his assets into gold reserves, or hiding out in the ark because he was gone.

What brought about the Great Flood of Noah's day? The sixth chapter of Genesis contains references to "sons of God" who took "the daughters of men" as wives (Gen. 6:1–2). Scholars disagree over whether the "sons of God" were fallen angels or merely the sons of godly men who married the daughters of ungodly men. Either way, the antediluvians (the people who lived before the Great Flood) spawned a race of powerful giants and a society of evil. If the depth of human depravity outlined in the New Testament describes what we escaped through Jesus' death and resurrection, then Enoch's generation must have been worse (Gen. 6:4–5)! That generation was so evil that God decided He would destroy it and start over.

The human race went in opposite directions after Adam and Eve were ejected from the Garden of Eden. The fourth and fifth chapters of the book of Genesis provide a picture of Adam's lineage through his two surviving sons: Cain and Seth (who replaced Abel after Cain murdered him).

Most of us hurry past the Bible's genealogies (or the "begats") as fast as we can, but gold is hidden in those verses if we dig below the surface. The genealogies of Cain and Seth offer us a treasure of godly insight and prophetic truth.

If you carefully compare the next two scripture passages, you will notice something odd about the way God's Word keeps these two genealogical records:

CAIN'S LINE

Cain went out from the presence of the LORD, and dwelt in the land of Nod, on the east of Eden. And Cain knew his wife; and she conceived, and bare Enoch [*not Enoch of Seth's line*]: and he builded a city, and called the name of the city, after the name of his son, Enoch. And unto Enoch was born Irad: and Irad begat Mehujael: and Mehujael begat Methusael: and Methusael begat Lamech. (Gen. 4:16–18, italics mine)

SETH'S LINE

Adam lived an hundred and thirty years, and begat a son in his own likeness, after his image; and called his name Seth . . . And all the days that Adam lived were nine hundred and thirty years: *and he died*. And *Seth lived* an hundred and five years, and begat Enos: and *Seth lived* after he begat Enos eight hundred and seven years . . . *and he died*. And *Enos lived* ninety years, and begat Cainan: and *Enos lived* after he begat Cainan eight hundred and fifteen years . . . *and he died*. And *Cainan lived* seventy years, and begat Mahalaleel: *and Cainan lived* after he begat Mahalaleel eight hundred and forty years . . . *and he died*. And *Mahalaleel lived* sixty and five years, and begat Jared: and *Mahalaleel lived* after he begat Jared eight hundred and thirty years . . . and *he died*. And *Jared lived* an hundred sixty and two years, and he begat Enoch: and *Jared lived* after he begat Enoch eight hundred years . . . and *he died*. And *Enoch lived* sixty and five years, and begat Methuselah: and *Enoch walked with God* after he begat Methuselah three hundred years, and begat sons and daughters: and all the days of Enoch were three hundred sixty and five years: *and Enoch walked with God: and he was not; for God took him.* (Gen. 5:3, 5–24, italics mine)

CAIN'S LINE: THE SINFUL REMNANT
EXTRACTED FROM THE GARDEN

When the Bible describes the ancestral line of Cain, it talks about their great cities and personal accomplishments. They were people of the world, the remnant of sinful man extracted and evacuated from the Garden of Eden. They were sinful beyond description, yet they were also people of knowledge and worldly understanding (which speaks volumes about the value of "educating" people out of their sin).

Educated and successful or not, those people were so devoted to personal pleasure, entertainment, and lustful abominations that God Himself came down only seven generations after Adam and said, "I am going to destroy the whole race and start over. It has gone too far to salvage."

ENOCH'S COUNTERPART WAS A PROUD
MURDERER AND POLYGAMIST

If you count seven generations from Adam in Cain's line, you end up with Lamech, the proud double-murderer and polygamist who refused to forgive or repent of his sin. *He represented the world gone mad and the prelude to the Flood of Noah.* He was the "cousin" of Enoch the preacher's son. Lamech was the poster child of Cain's proud, violent, self-indulgent, and lawless lineage. He was the pride of Cain's line, the dark seed of a murderous rebel.

SETH'S LINE: THE RIGHTEOUS REMNANT

Adam's third son, Seth, evidently followed in Abel's footsteps and had a heart after God. When Seth's son, Enos, was born, the Bible notes, "Then began men to call upon the name of the LORD" (Gen. 4:26). If you count seven generations from Adam in Seth's line through Enos, you end up with Enoch, the man who walked with God.

Seven is the biblical number of completion and perfection, and the two men, Enoch and Lamech, clearly represent the completion of what their forefathers began. Seven is also the number of fulfillment and consummation. A period of unavoidable tension between time and destiny and sin and righteousness was quickly approaching, with the inevitable consummation of judgment.

God always has more to say about the righteous than He does about the wicked. The wicked are not even a thought in the mind of God. The Bible passage in Genesis 4 devotes only three verses to the lineage of Cain. Not so for the righteous!

SETH'S "BEGATS" REVEAL A HINT OF GLORY TO COME

The world (and many Christians as well) seems to think that "the eyes of the Lord are running to and fro throughout the whole earth to find someone to whack with a baseball bat" (to terribly misquote the passage in 2 Chron. 16:9). This is how it really reads: "For the eyes of the LORD run to and fro throughout the whole earth, *to show himself strong in the behalf of them whose heart is perfect toward him*." We see the evidence for this truth in Seth's "begats" in Genesis 5.

Adam lived 930 years and saw half of his family walk with God and the other half do their best to create hell on earth. If you look closely at the verses describing Seth, you will see that he *lived* 105 years "and begat Enos: and Seth *lived*" (Gen. 5:6–8).

What about Enos? He *lived*, witnessed the birth of his son, Cainan, and then we read that he *lived* again and finally died (Gen. 5:9–11). We read the same thing for everyone in Seth's line until Enoch breaks the pattern and checks out of this world early to be with God.

This is the first hint of the *rebirth* you and I enjoy in Christ this very moment! Let me paint my favorite picture for you. Somewhere in the pavilions of glory, you will find *your name* signed on the canvas of eternity with a heavenly quill pen dipped in the precious blood of God's own Son.

I can tell you that you will find my name there, too, recorded in God's unequaled script: January 13, 1957, Rod Parsley *lived*. Eight years later, you will see that God took out His pen and the scarlet ink of life to record my name once more on the hallowed pages of another book called the Lamb's Book of Life, writing: Rod Parsley *lived again*. In that year, I had an encounter with the God of eternity, and my life was changed forever.

In the historical record of the almighty God, I lived not once but twice. I am living my *second* life right now through my rebirth in Christ.

ENOCH LIVED "ON THE BRINK" AS WE DO!

Enoch is especially fascinating to me because he lived "on the brink" as we do! He knew what it was like to sense in the deepest part of his being that something big was about to happen. Anybody in our generation who is willing to tell even just a little bit of the truth will admit he senses an ominous weight or pressure all around him. It is almost like the calm you sense before a big, gutter-busting thunderstorm is about to descend on you.

Enoch lived under that "calamity canopy" all of his life. Things were supposedly going better than ever, but he could sense a shift in the winds of time. Things seemed to be out of joint in some way. Something or someone was about to snap the universe back into its proper place, and somehow he sensed it was going to be a violent adjustment.

Today, you and I are living with a nagging sense that major change is around the corner. If you have ever built a house of cards, then you know that the higher and fancier you get, the more unstable the structure becomes. Even the slightest jar or puff of wind can cause the entire house of cards to collapse.

Our economy may seem to boom for six or seven years straight, but what is it built upon? Is it built upon unshakable biblical principles of investment in long-term value, ethical business practices, and the innate value of life? Or is the economy built upon the foundation of greed and the rapid accumulation of wealth at any cost? Your answer tells you whether the national and international economic structure is a solid house built upon a firm foundation or a house of cards built upon shifting sands. Either way, the house is about to experience life in a wind tunnel.

COLLAPSE WAS INEVITABLE

Enoch lived in a society that resembled a great and magnificent house of cards. It was based upon the shaky foundations of man's strengths, sensual appetites, and open rebellion against God and His ways. The collapse was inevitable. The only questions were: When? How? and How many people will be affected?

My fascination with Enoch concerns God's "journal entries" about his life and sudden disappearance from the scene before the great storm arrived to rearrange human history and permanently alter the earth's geography. It may seem repetitive, but bear with me as we look once again at God's record of Enoch's abnormal life cycle before the Great Flood:

> Enoch lived sixty and five years, and begat Methuselah: and Enoch walked with God after he begat Methuselah three hundred years, and begat sons and daughters: and all the days of Enoch were three hundred sixty and five years: and *Enoch walked with God: and he was not; for God took him.* (Gen. 5:21–24, italics mine)

By faith Enoch was translated that he should not see death; and *was not found,* because God had translated him: *for before his translation he had this testimony, that he pleased God.* (Heb. 11:5, italics mine)

Woe unto them! for *they have gone in the way of Cain,* and ran greedily after the error of Balaam for reward, and perished in the gainsaying of Korah. These [people in the church] are spots in your feasts of charity, when they feast with you, feeding themselves without fear: clouds they are without water, carried about of winds; trees whose fruit withereth, without fruit, twice dead, plucked up by the roots; raging waves of the sea, foaming out their own shame; wandering stars, to whom is reserved the blackness of darkness for ever. *And Enoch also, the seventh from Adam, prophesied of these,* saying, *Behold, the Lord cometh with ten thousands of his saints, to execute judgment upon all.* (Jude 11–15, italics mine)

REVELATION TAILORED FOR A GENERATION LIVING ON THE BRINK

What a Book! It is amazing to me that God would bury such a prophetic treasure of divine insight into the final moments of human history in the middle of some "begats" in the first book of the Bible. Then He confirmed it thousands of years later in the New Testament. The revelation of Enoch, the man who walked with God, is like a diamond displayed in all of its brilliance on the velvet couch of human history—especially for *the generation living on the brink* as he did. All we need are eyes to see.

Just a few generations after Enoch left the earth to continue his walk with God in the heavenlies, the world known to mankind was suddenly destroyed in the Great Deluge. What did God do with a man who walked with Him before the destruction came? He *took* him!

Did you notice that God didn't take everyone who "called upon the name of the LORD"? He didn't even take all of the people named in Seth's genealogy. They may have been good people who "went to church" as the pew sitters of that day. They may have given offerings or prayed prayers from time to time. It didn't matter because when it was time for God to save whatever needed to be pulled out of the storm of judgment about to descend on the earth, He sought only one man (and made provisions to preserve the family of one other, Noah).

ENOCH'S TESTIMONY: HE PLEASED GOD

God's Word presents us with a proposition: Why not walk with Him now? Enoch lived a godly life in an ungodly generation character-ized by an overt rejection of God and His ways. When a divine hand removed him, somebody must have been looking for Enoch because the writer of Hebrews implied that whoever was looking for him didn't find him (Heb. 11:5).

The Bible also says Enoch's unique testimony in a time of worldwide sinfulness was that he "pleased God." He accomplished in the decayed society of his era what you and I strive to do in our own day: he received the witness that he had *pleased God.*

THERE IS A DIVINE *DISINTEREST* IN MAN'S ACCOMPLISHMENTS

God is still looking for people who know how to please Him, and He still displays an amazing level of *disinterest* in all of the accom-plishments of man's hand. He could care less about our buildings, our bank accounts, our yachts, our college degrees, or our sports achievements. He insists on asking each of us the same irritating question Jesus put to the people of another generation who were living "in the fullness of time":

For what shall it profit a man, if he shall gain the whole world, and lose his own soul? Or what shall a man give in exchange for his soul? Whosoever therefore shall be ashamed of me and of my words in this adulterous and sinful generation; of him also shall the Son of man be ashamed, when he cometh in the glory of his Father with the holy angels. (Mark 8:36–38)

Enoch had a testimony that he pleased God. He also had a testimony for doing something else that very few Christians today can honestly claim. According to the book of Jude, Enoch prophesied and preached to his generation about the coming of the Lord "with ten thousands of his saints, to execute judgment upon all" (Jude 14–15). That is definitely at the top of our politically incorrect list for the new millennium, but it was even less "PC" (politically correct) in Enoch's day. He didn't let that stop him, and God blessed him for it.

Can you see any parallel between our postmillennium generation and the pre-Flood generation of Enoch's day? Are we technologically advanced? Is our society lawless, sexually promiscuous, and spiritually bankrupt? Do we call good evil while calling evil good?

My friend, people who live on the brink can't afford to go through the motions of life as if everything is normal. Things are *not* normal. Above all, *we* are not normal. As the Scriptures declare, we are "the sons of God, without rebuke, in the midst of a crooked and perverse nation, among whom [we] shine as lights in the world; holding forth the word of life" (Phil. 2:15–16).

Our witness must shine as brightly to our generation as Enoch's did before the Great Flood! We must go about it the same way Enoch did it—by *walking with God* and pleasing Him. As always, the finger of God points first to the shepherds and then to His sheep.

CHAPTER 2

THE BLAME SHIFTERS
AND THE
REMNANT PREACHERS

Millions of people are asking, "Where did all of the violence come from? Why are our children killing one another in their schools, neighborhoods, and city streets? How can our own Supreme Court set aside our most basic moral foundations and religious freedoms and still call it justice? Why are so many people suffering from a national epidemic of chronic neuroses, syndromes, and phobias? Who decided it was acceptable to broadcast violent and sexually oriented television programming during family viewing hours?"

Some blame the chaos exclusively on Hollywood, on the left-leaning news media, or on some violence-ridden video game. Others try to pin all of the responsibility on a rock-and-roll record or particular recording artists or groups. It is my conviction that our nation's headlong plunge into sin, sexual permissiveness, violence, and the glorification of rebellion *can be laid at the feet of our preachers!* (No, I didn't make a mistake in my choice of words.) Sin and depravity dominate our society because the church has no gospel.

If you would like to lay an indictment somewhere, then lay it at the base of a powerless pulpit. As the preacher goes, so goes the church. As the church goes, so goes the nation. As the nation goes, so goes the world. That is why I am compelled to include this chapter on preachers in a book that will be read primarily by people who are not preachers. If I can help you understand the pressures and temptations faced by preachers, you will be better equipped to support and pray for the preachers God brings into your life.

Half of what we hear on Christian television, I'm sad to say, is nothing more than dressed up Eastern mysticism or self-help humanism. These programs teach us how to meditate and how to be a success in the eyes of the world. They teach us how to be people of great intellectual ability by "recognizing all that is within us."

Jesus told us what was within us. He said, "For out of the heart proceed evil thoughts, murders, adulteries, fornications, thefts, false witness, blasphemies" (Matt. 15:19). Let me tell you that the only good thing in you is what God put in you, fixed or cleansed in you. Everything else is questionable.

IF THERE IS SOMETHING GOOD IN US, THEN GOD PUT IT THERE

That is the reason your Bible says the sharing of our faith is energized by the acknowledgment of every good thing that is in us *by Christ Jesus* (Philem. 1:6). The only good things within us are those things born of God's Word, of His Spirit, and of His kingdom. God says we should acknowledge that truth, give heed to it, and put it in the forefront. In other words, it is time to stop talking about *you, me,* and *us* and focus on *Him* for a change!

My wife, Joni, asked me a question that I just can't get out of my mind. She said, "Why are preachers always talking about improving our self-image when God said we ought to crucify ourselves and the lust thereof?"

I don't think half the preachers in America have that testimony.

They're not warning anybody of judgment to come. They're trying to teach somebody a self-help program. We have stripped our Bibles of everything that smacks of negativity because that isn't politically correct.

My friend, we need to rediscover what the Bible calls the *fear of God* and its large-scale cousin in God's plan: *judgment*. America will not escape God's justice. Do you think any people or nation on earth can disrespect the things of God, mock His commandments, laugh in the face of His direction, and then escape justice? We aren't talking about some shoddy court of men. We are talking about the unswerving justice meted out by the God who knows all things and cannot allow sin of any kind in His presence.

The church's circuitous path to political correctness has brought us the fawning acceptance of man in every social and political circle, but it has failed to win God's approval. Presidents call church leaders for advice (until they don't like what is said). Television journalists call Christian leaders for positive sound bites, and national magazines call us for tasty quotes on the latest "warm and fuzzy" issues. If you are really doing things right, your mayor may give you the key to the city.

Why didn't the apostle Paul ever get one of those keys? The only key he got was the one hanging on a jailer's side as they threw his beaten and battered carcass into an inner prison. When our big-name preachers walk into town, they expect to receive the keys to the city. When Paul walked into a town or city, he expected to get up close and personal with the local prison cell or at least a rock shower or two.

PAUL GOT STONED AND FINNEY GOT DEAD CATS

Something is amiss here. It used to be that America's best preachers were greeted with a barrage of dead cats or a hail of bullets. When Charles G. Finney preached the gospel, people actually threw dead cats at him. The ministry of a young and unknown preacher named Billy Graham caught the nation's eye only after a man tried to shoot him during an early California tent revival meeting. Some of our modern-day wonders won't preach unless somebody throws thousand-dollar bills in their direction first!

America's sleepy-headed and half-seduced preachers are in for a rude awakening by the Holy Spirit. The harvest is near, and this is not the time to go to sleep in Zion. I love preachers too much to leave them slumbering. I'm determined to do everything I can do to shake them and stick them back in a pulpit armed with the authority God gave them when He ordained them in the first place.

Edmund Burke observed, "The only thing necessary for the triumph of evil is for good men to do nothing." That goes double for preachers. This is no time for us to sit down and moan and groan, or to deliver saccharine-sweet psychological solutions to spiritual problems.

Too many "professional" pastors spend their time searching psychology magazines for the newest phobias, conditions, and syndromes (or "sin-dromes") to help them mollify the guilt and justify the sins that so easily beset their sheep and perpetual counselees. They are looking for the latest psychological scapegoats to help carry away the weight of sin's guilt without challenging the sinners.

BLAME SHIFTERS ALWAYS LOOK FOR SCAPEGOATS

We live in a society of blame shifters. It is acceptable to find scapegoats such as parents, teachers, principals, or judges, and blame them for "making us go bad" in various areas of our lives. It is the politically correct thing to do on pop psychology talk shows, on political commentary programs, in church Sunday school classes, and in our pulpits.

But God has never been baffled by our rambling blame sessions or blanket excuses, "The devil made me do it." The devil didn't make you do anything; he made a suggestion, and *you* made the thought a deed.

There are no corroborating witnesses, prosecutors, jury members, or public defenders in His court. He knows and sees all things—and He remembers with perfection. Only the blood of the Lamb can cause God to "forget" (our sins that is). There is only one Advocate, the risen Christ; but He defends only humble, blood-washed members of His body. He leaves the proud to their own devices.

The bad news is that we must own or admit and accept our guilt and take personal responsibility as sinners before we can benefit from the good news. The good news is that the sacrificed Lamb of God has already paid the penalty for us and He has taken away our sin and guilt once and for all. God's cure for sin comes only through the door of the blood of the Lamb, the cross of Christ, and total death to self associated with true repentance from sin. (I wish to God that some colleagues would throw away their psychology books and get themselves some Bibles.)

Our nation has deteriorated to its present condition because we have had *powerless pulpits* for far too long! Where the uncompromised Word of God is preached with anointing, conviction, and a lifestyle to match, every evil influence must yield to the divine force of righteousness.

A NEGLIGENT BRAVE MAN IS NO BETTER THAN A DESERTING COWARD

Power concedes nothing without a demand. Therefore, the ultimate control of any dictator is directly linked to the endurance of those people whom he seeks to oppress.[1] A brave man negligent of his office is of no more virtue than the coward who deserts in the time of gravest danger.[2] It is time for God's preachers to stand up and *preach!*

What is a preacher? A preacher is *the voice through which the heart of God delivers the purpose of the infinite into the realm of the finite with all the power proper to its need.* I am a preacher.

We are at an undeniable point of crisis in the early moments of a new millennium. Our culture is in chaos because the moral foundations constructed by the tenets of our faith are crumbling around us. We are at a crossroads, or what Andy Grove, chairman of the board of the Intel Corporation, calls a "strategic inflection point" of infinite importance.[3]

When the pressures of change reach a point where they force a "change or shift of standards," you have reached a strategic inflection point. In the business world, the companies that are able to perceive change and adapt to it will continue to grow. The companies that resist change and stand immovable will be crushed by the irresistible weight of change. Over the ages, churches have rarely, if ever, been ready for change, and history records the disastrous results.

At the time strategic inflection points surface, we are faced with a critical decision between choices that *seem* to be very close together. However, what seems to be a small thing ends up taking us in a direction diametrically opposed to the direction we would have been going. This is where the church is today. A polarization is taking place between casual Christianity (modeled nationwide by the First Church of the Lukewarm Pew Sitters) and committed believers who will put their lives on the line for the sake of Christ.

GOD USES PREACHERS TO TAKE US
BY THE NAPE OF THE NECK

We are faced with a choice, but at the same time we are entangled in a fatal complacency. When our complacency exceeds our desire for change, the consequence is concession and chaos. This is where preachers are vital to our survival! God uses anointed preachers to take us by the spiritual nape of the neck and drag us up in front of His Word.

Teachers serve the valuable purpose in the church of feeding the flock of God with a steady supply of God's Word. By nature, the teacher's ministry is instructive and geared toward filling the heart and head with truth.

However, the Bible says that when God's people sit and feast on the Word but refuse to do what it says, they become "like unto a man beholding his natural face in a glass: for he beholdeth himself, and goeth his way, and straightway forgetteth what manner of man he was" (James 1:23–24).

Preachers also feed the flock with God's Word, but they constantly *confront* us with the convicting truth of God's Word, causing us to conform our lifestyles to His will instead of our own. Preaching demands a certain *forcefulness* that will never be classified as politically correct or win popularity contests.

I fear for the preacher who says, "I have three hundred people now. They pay me really well and get me a new car every year. Why on earth would I want to say anything that might offend them?" My friend, the ultimate end of political correctness is political chaos and anarchy, when every man does as he sees fit.

How can God's people grow when week after week, they waltz into God's house fifteen minutes late to hear some guy whose pants are entirely too tight play some "Bela Lugosi" music on an organ and then listen to a so-called preacher pump out three points and a poem? Our songs lack emotion and conviction. We produce nothing more than a memorized shout, a taught tongue, and a learned dance. There is not enough power in our services to get anybody in the building saved, much less healed and delivered!

Rebellion against church leaders seems almost justified when even the preacher can't seem to keep *Playboy* out from underneath his car seat. Rebellion against church leaders seems almost justified when too many leaders are caught lying, manipulating, or practicing fraud and thievery in a flaky money-raising scheme.

Who is going to save this generation?

Where have all the preachers gone?

Who will declare the doctrine to the church?

Who will lay their lives down to repair the breach?

Anyone who dares to say, "I think I'll take that challenge," will feel the need of God's help as he has never felt it before. I fought the call as a young high school graduate more than two decades ago. I knew it wasn't glamorous. I knew it was a call to hard work, thankless toil, confrontation, misunderstanding, and a lifelong dedication to discipline and holiness in the sight of God.

I didn't come from a long line of preachers; I came from a family of faithful, dedicated, and quiet church workers and lay ministers. In high school, I felt I was called to preach, but *I never did anything about it.* I wanted to take a year off from school after I graduated, so I tried my hand at a number of jobs in Columbus, Ohio.

Eventually I answered the call, and others must do the same. *We stand on the brink of cataclysmic change in a new millennium!* It is marked by untold masses of people who are lost, confused, and damned unless they hear and receive the good news. Heaven is once again searching for that rare commodity called a preacher:

Whosoever shall call upon the name of the Lord shall be saved. How then shall they call on him in whom they have not believed? and how shall they believe in him of whom they have not heard? and *how shall they hear without a preacher?* (Rom. 10:13–14, italics mine)

If mankind ever needed the saving, prodding, exhorting, and convicting ministry of the preacher, it is now. "Do what we cannot do, Lord! And give us the courage to do what we *must* do!"

I KNOW WHY GOD "PLANTED" ME
IN AN OHIO CORNFIELD

After more than two decades of ministry, I am more aware of my assignment than I have ever been. I've begun to understand why God called and anointed me to raise up a place such as World Harvest Church and Breakthrough Media Ministries—right in the middle of a cornfield in the central United States so far away from the Bible Belt.

I have surrendered to the revelation of my assignment before God. The prophet Isaiah described it this way: "And they that shall be of thee shall build the old waste places: thou shalt raise up the foundations of many generations; and thou shalt be called, The repairer of the breach, The restorer of paths to dwell in" (Isa. 58:12).

God is searching the earth for called, anointed, and ordained preachers. They are a dying breed. He wants people like Shadrach, Meshach, and Abednego, who would not bow and could not burn. He is looking for somebody like Stephen who will declare, "Stone me at midnight, and I'll still have a song."

PILLOW YOUR HEAD IN THE SHAGGY
MANE OF THE LION

God wants another Daniel, a man who will say, "Throw me in the lions' den. I'll reckon my position, turn my face toward Jerusalem, offer my prayer to God, pillow my head in the shaggy mane of the lion, and sleep like a baby all night long." We need an army of preachers who will stand with Paul, who told his young disciple, Timothy:

> For the which cause I also suffer these things: nevertheless I am not ashamed: for I know whom I have believed, and am persuaded

that he is able to keep that which I have committed unto him against that day. Hold fast the form of sound words, which thou hast heard of me, in faith and love which is in Christ Jesus. That good thing which was committed unto thee keep by the Holy Ghost which dwelleth in us. (2 Tim. 1:12–14)

A genuine preacher is not a puppet, nor is he a mere pulpiteer with the silvery-tongued eloquence of a great orator. A preacher is not a pleaser given to spoon-feeding the listeners small portions of bland pabulum. A preacher declares the truth of God's Word with genuine authority that is based on the bedrock of personal morality. (It's been so long since some of us have seen one that we don't rightly know what one looks like.)

The greatest preachers in this nation probably don't have their faces plastered all over television. Most of us haven't heard their names, but they have become the guardians of the souls of humanity. God is looking for candidates who are praying, "God, if You call me to fifteen people in the backwoods somewhere, I'll be thankful. If nobody ever knows my name or asks me to preach at a big meeting; if I never appear on a television program or hear my voice broadcast on a radio program, I will be faithful. The only One who *must* know my name is You, Lord. If You call me to pastor, I will be faithful to the end."

A GOOD WORD FOR GOOD MEN
READY TO DO SOMETHING

To rephrase Edmund Burke, "The only way for evil to triumph as it has in America is for good men to do nothing." The best men in America are not in politics or education. The best men in America are not bouncing a round ball up and down a hardwood floor or occupying the revered academic chairs of university science departments. The best men in America can be found faithfully delivering the Word of the Lord from behind the sacred desk or on their knees seeking a fresh word from the infinite, almighty God. They have power and courage to deliver with divine authority, "Thus saith the Spirit of the Lord!"

Stop hanging your head, Preacher. Stop being made to feel like a second-class citizen. Stop being made to feel by some "minister" of this world's religious order that you are not good enough. Forget about all of that because you possess something that he will never find. He's always seeking but never able to come to the knowledge of the truth.

A true preacher deals with the absolute truth of God's Word. He lets nothing stop him. He doesn't back up because "Dr. Yea Yea" strokes his goatee and his smoke encircles a wreath around his head and says Jesus never lived. It doesn't matter if you finished only the seventh grade. If God called you and put His word in you, you're the smartest man walking this planet.

Kingdoms will crumble with all of their monuments. Societies will collapse, and governments will topple. Armies will be defeated, but the work of the remnant preacher must go on.

Now for the other side of the equation. Preacher, know that men and women will spend the endless ages of eternity in the bowels of a devil's hell or in the pavilions of the grandeur and the glory of almighty God *based upon your words* and *your life*. We are the living epistles of God, known and read of all men. And though you shout loud with your words, your life is drowning them out.

Where, oh, where have all the preachers gone? Where are some Johns, some sons of thunder? God isn't looking for preachers with manicured nails. He wants preachers who will dare to be like Jesus, who are willing to stick their arms elbow deep into the muck and mire of humanity to extract helpless, hopeless, dying, destitute souls and to give their lives for them if necessary.

ARE YOU READY TO GO TO HELL FOR SOMEBODY?

Paul was ready. He said, "I would rather be cast into hell than for them not to hear my preaching." If you went to seminary, how many of your fellow graduates declared that they were ready to go to hell for somebody? Most of the time, you can't talk to a pastor without going through fourteen secretaries! Time and again, I return to this powerful quote, which I paraphrased from statements made by Will Durant, who lived from 1885 to 1981:

> There's no greater drama than a few remnant preachers scorned by a succession of adversaries, bearing trials with tenacity, multiplying miraculously, building order in chaos, all the while rescuing the despondent, redeeming the downtrodden, and reviving the life of Christ in the hearts of humanity. Oh they're beaten and battered, but they are not bowed.

Preacher, it is not your job to please people. It is not your job to make them feel good. It is not your job to increase their self-esteem. Again, why should we try to increase the esteem of a "self" that God commands us to crucify?

God, give us preachers who will preach the uncompromised Word and won't have to ask folks at denominational headquarters what they think about it. Give us preachers who won't have to ask their spouses, in-laws, and outlaws what they think about it.

SO YOU WANT TO PREACH: WHERE IS YOUR ALTAR?

All it takes to be what most of us call a preacher is a sermon and a halfway developed gift of gab. I'm not talking about that kind of preacher. If you want to be a real preacher, you are going to have an altar somewhere.

Much can be done quickly when Christ is the center. If we can stop talking about *me, my ministry, you, your ministry,* or *my word, my plan, my program,* and *my intellect* and center our lives and ministry on the risen Christ, we will see thousands, hundreds of thousands, and even millions saved, healed, and delivered in His name.

We need to take a lesson from God's design of our solar system. Each planet in the system is held in place by the delicate balance between the gravitational pull of the sun at the center and the speed and outward inertial force of its orbit. There is a clear order to the system, and Mercury is the first planet or the one closest to the sun.

Mercury goes around the sun in only 88 days while it takes Earth 365 days to orbit our star. Mercury, the wing-footed planet, is so close to the center that the temperatures on its surface average an estimated 333 degrees Fahrenheit.

Earth is in the third position from the sun, and is perfectly positioned to sustain life. If we were closer to the sun, we would burn up. If we were farther from the sun, we would freeze to death. The planet farthest from the sun is a frozen ball of gases named Pluto that spends 248 earth years circling the sun just once. It can't sustain life because it is too far removed from the sun in the center.

The church has moved so far away from the Son as its center that it takes three thousand church members one full year to win one person to Jesus! I have news for you: we are getting closer to His return, and the closer we get to Him, the faster things are going to happen. We will see more healings, miracles, and supernatural acts of deliverance in one year than most of us have seen in a lifetime.

What took me more than twenty years to build, you might be able to build in only twenty months. What it takes you twenty months to build, another might accomplish in only two days. Am I out of my mind? I have one name, one day, and one number for you to consider: Peter, pentecost, and three thousand.

WHAT CAN GOD DO WITH YOU?

If God birthed a church of more than three thousand in one day early in the first century, why wouldn't He do it now? If He used an uneducated commercial fisherman with a hot temper and a poor performance record to harvest three thousand souls in one day, what can He do with you?

Whatever you do, don't start preaching for results. It will make you drift off track. God never called anyone to preach for results. He calls each one of us to say *what* He tells us to say, *when* He tells us to say it, *how* He tells us to say it, and *to whom* He sends us. Anything less is disobedience. Results are none of our business. That is God's department alone.

If God calls you to preach, then you need to go to the pulpit as if it were a cross. Preach the Word as if you are a dying man with nothing to lose, who is preaching to other dying men. Preach as if there is no tomorrow; preach as if it will be your last opportunity to stop somebody from going to hell. If it makes the crowds come, make sure it means nothing to you. If everybody leaves, make sure it means nothing to you. Just preach His Word and leave the results to Him.

God has had a remnant in every generation. Somewhere, He still has an Elijah and an Elisha ready in the wings. He still has a Shadrach, a Meshach, and an Abednego. He still has three thousand who have not yet bowed their knees to Baal.

THE WORST INDICTMENT OF ALL

When Christian television programs first hit the airwaves, there were no Christian stations to speak of. We had choices of ABC, NBC, and CBS. Every TV set had rabbit ears, and you had to actually get up from the sofa to change the channel on the television set—with your *own hand*. On Sunday mornings from seven o'clock until noon you could tune into any of those stations and you would find a preacher calling America out of its sin-sick condition. That went by the wayside with "progress."

Largely used as a tool of evangelism in its infancy, Christian television then "graduated" to the production of the Christian celebrity.

All of a sudden with the celebrity came a desire to keep the crowd. So we replaced preaching primarily with the fivefold ministry office gift of teaching. Even there, we had to be careful because our audience was much broader. People who believed in the Trinity dared not preach it on television lest some people who didn't believe in the Trinity stop supporting their ministry.

You don't know what most Christian television personalities really believe because most of them won't tell you. Most of the nationally known television preachers are pentecostal or charismatic in persuasion, and they believe in the doctrine of the baptism of the Holy Spirit as a second experience. When was the last time you heard one of them preach on the baptism of the Holy Spirit or pray on television for people to receive the baptism of the Holy Spirit? You probably can't name it. When was the last time you heard a solid message on sin?

CELEBRITY PREACHERS OFTEN PRODUCE SPIRITUAL PABULUM

Celebrity preachers have reduced what is projected through the camera to the masses to little more than spiritual baby pabulum. I heard one not long ago "preach" on "how to put our shopping cart back." Every Christian magazine you see is packed with advertisements for marriage seminar after marriage seminar. Why do Holy Spirit–filled, fire-baptized believers need marriage seminars? That is elementary. Why must the body of Christ be taught how to pray? Nobody taught the Christians in the book of Acts how to pray.

The true preacher does not deal in the merchandise of the surface and extremities. The gospel preacher puts his hand on the heart of humanity and announces, "If I can get your heart right, then I won't worry about adultery and theft, and I won't have to teach you how to give, how to be healed, or how to pray."

We're dealing on the surface because we're afraid to dive into the heart of the matter. We must be as Samuel who, as a lone man standing on a mountain, pointed his finger at a nation and a people and announced, "You are wrong!"

Let me tell you what it takes to be on TV. Whenever I've gone to ABC—or any Christian station for that matter—not once have I been asked whether I was anointed or called. No one asked me whether I had a word from God or verified the moral standards of my personal life. The only thing they ask me is this: "*Can you pay the bill?*"

The bottom line is that I can broadcast my programs on as many stations as I can pay for. I could spend $10 million next week and not bat an eye, and no one would ask me whether I loved my wife. If you pay the bill, you can be a TV star. The tragedy is that we think this is the winning formula to "win America."

I AM NOT THE GUARDIAN OF YOUR SOUL— THAT IS YOUR LOCAL PASTOR'S JOB

No matter how many times my face is seen on America's television screens, I am not the guardian of your soul. Your *local pastor* is the God-ordained guardian of your soul, not some television preacher. God intends to do everything He does through the apostolic authority of the local church in this hour.

Local pastors watch the Christian celebrities preaching pabulum on television, they see the large following they attract, and they equate that with success! The next step is that they think they have to preach the same kind of sermons the preaching stars preach to a national audience. They end up preaching nothing but pabulum, ear-tickling philosophies, and vain deceits too.

We need to realize that the *assignment* is different. I am both a local pastor and a national television preacher. I don't preach to the members of my congregation in the same way that I preach to people in another pastor's church or to my television viewers across the nation. In my local church, God holds me responsible as the guardian of the souls of His sheep. He holds me responsible to preach sound doctrine, whether it goes down smoothly or not. I have to preach eternal judgment, repentance from dead works, the doctrine of baptism, holiness, and the truth about the end times.

Pastor, I declare to you under God that you must be a man of God. Your number one assignment is to get alone with God and receive a message in secret that He declares through you in public. You have no right to watch somebody else and try to imitate or emulate what he says. Your job is to step out before your spiritual flock and declare, "Thus saith the Spirit of the Lord!"

So you want to be a preacher? Yes, you can be a preacher if you want to weep until you can cry no more. Preach the Word if you are willing to have your heart break into a million pieces and risk seeing your family members forsake you and your friends turn their backs on you. Do you want to be misunderstood and laughed at? Preach the Word without compromise. Do you want the newspapers in your city to write your accolades or flaming missiles? It depends on whether you want to be a preacher or a man pleaser.

IF YOU ARE NOT CALLED TO PREACH, THEN DON'T

If you can do anything else and be happy, then *do it*. I beg you, do it. Sell cars or real estate. Be a banker or go into politics. Do anything but preach if you are not truly called by God.

God's message in the new millennium is the same as it was in the previous millennium: "The soul that sinneth, it shall die." Do you go to bed hearing the cries of the perishing? Do their groanings wake you? Does the thought of their perishing make you walk the floor, or is the gospel just a business to you? Don't step behind the sacred desk if you see the ministry as a vocation that amounts to another way to pay your bills.

Maybe you already pastor a church. What would happen if you took a survey of your congregation to discover what they really know about God and His Word? Do they know about eternal judgment, or have you been afraid to mention it on Sunday mornings?

"PASTOR, PRAY FOR ME SO I WILL PREACH THE TRUTH AGAIN"

Are you preaching for results? I preached in a church not long ago where the preacher thanked me and then said as he wept, "I used to preach like that, but then I started getting invited to a lot of big meetings." He said, "You know that if you preach a popular message that is trite and trivial, thousands of people will scream, clap, laugh, and jump for joy. It's intoxicating to know that they like you." Then the preacher looked at me with tears streaming down his face and said, "Pastor, pray for me so I will preach the truth again. I need God's help because it is so hard to preach the truth."

If I can't preach what God tells me to preach on our nation's broadcast stations and networks, then I will stand in the pulpit of my church and preach. It doesn't matter. I'm not going to compromise. There is room for teaching the body of Christ and there is room for all types of ministry, but if you really look, everybody seems to have gone the same way.

How about a message on holiness? How about a message on the sin of divorce or Jesus' warning that any man who looks at a woman with lust has committed adultery? Now wouldn't that go over big on

Christian TV? Do you see how far we've come? People almost laugh when a man says, "I've been married to this woman for forty-two years."

It's not hard to live right. It's not hard to love God with all your heart. It's time to come out from among them and be separate. O God, give us a few preachers. Give us a few to point the direction.

If you are a pastor, called to the ministry, remember that God is not calling you to be like anybody else. Nobody can do what you can do. Whoever He's given you to be the guardian of their souls, would you sell out for them right now? Will you be faithful even if you never mount a platform with more than five hundred people in attendance? Will you say what God wants you to say and do it in love? Make up your mind to speak God's Word and leave the results to Him.

He calls ministers to be shepherds. That is not a call to luxury; it is a call to toil, to labor, to sacrifice, and to pain. The pastor who sends the sheep out to test the water is not a shepherd but a hireling and no lover of the sheep. The Good Shepherd sends only true shepherds to tend His sheep as if they were their own.

CHAPTER 3

THE SPIRIT OF THE AGE

A divine discontent stirs in my spirit as never before. The Holy Spirit has revived the compelling force of well-known scripture passages I thought I had mastered. Now they burn anew in my heart with an unquenchable fire. I hear the prophet's proclamation in the night: "Cry aloud, spare not, lift up thy voice like a trumpet, and show my people their transgression, and the house of Jacob their sins" (Isa. 58:1).

America is rolling in unprecedented luxury and prosperity. She revels in excess and rollicks in pleasure, but in God's eyes, her immorality is revolting and she is rotting in her own sin. I suppose this is to be expected in a society where passions are nothing more than unbridled horses, where lust is exalted as lord, sin is elevated to sovereignty, Satan is worshiped as a saint, and man is magnified above his Maker.

The crisis is acute, the danger is imminent, and time is running out. Something must happen in the heart and soul of America before it is eternally too late. The choice is clear: we must repent or perish; we must choose Christ or chaos. The only question is, Which way will America go?

God is calling the body of Christ in this nation to impact society, but first we must rise above the blurry haze of indistinctiveness.

God is not calling us to play church or please the masses. He demands that we rise far above the status quo of "church normalcy." We have lived for so long in a society where "wrong is right" that true righteousness has become an abnormal thing.

God commended the remnant believers of Thyatira because they had not known the doctrine or the "depths of Satan" (Rev. 2:24). As for the other "church members," they were rebuked for accepting Jezebel's doctrine condoning adultery and a lifestyle of sin.

The devil has an inner circle of darkened hearts *in the church* to whom he imparted the mysteries (or "depths") of iniquity and degradation. Over a period of time, these doctors of damnation worked like leaven to permeate the mind-set of the body of Christ with relativism to the point that we now call evil good and good evil. If you doubt my words, turn on satellite TV or cable and watch Christian preachers for a while. Although some hold to the standard of God's Word, many do not.

A nation adrift is marked by its confused course through the priorities of life. Our nation preserves the whales of the sea, the whooping crane, and the snail darter, but our Supreme Court encourages profit-hungry abortionists to murder our unborn children with impunity under its immoral protection. First Amendment rights of free speech are quickly annulled if anyone mounts a public protest of the slaughter.

WE KNOW MORE AND UNDERSTAND LESS THAN EVER

As a people, we entered the new millennium smarter but not wiser. We know more and understand less than ever before. We go everywhere faster, but we end up nowhere. We can conquer space, but we can't seem to conquer our own lusts.

Our sin has opened a door for the spirit of the antichrist to unleash demon spirits as vessels of vengeance. They are wreaking havoc, killing, stealing, and destroying in every way conceivable. The schemes of international madmen such as Saddam Hussein and Slobodan Milosevic unwittingly work in league with the polished politicians in the White House and Congress who propagate perversion and pervert legislation on the home front. Street punks with assault rifles tucked inside long black trench coats are no more repulsive to the Lord than the so-called upstanding citizen who smugly shakes his fist at the commandments of a holy God.

The hard-core ranks of satanism's demonically deranged devotees now include high-profile recruits such as doctors, lawyers, politicians, and pop stars. *This onslaught of evil is too subtle, sinister, widespread, and far-reaching to be of human origin*. We are dealing with the carefully calculated conspiracy of demon spirits. Read the newspaper if you doubt my claim. The lengthy litany of unspeakable crimes committed by children as well as adults can be attributed only to the driving power of demonically inspired thoughts of destruction and compulsive acts of violence.

SOMETHING IS DRIVING OUR CHILDREN OVER THE BRINK

An evil supernatural force is driving our children over the brink. It may not show up in the standard curriculum for most university psychology departments, but that mystical, unusual, supernatural force is called a demon. The spirit of the world is concerned with the ordering of human beings and human affairs by demonic influence. The apostle Paul warned us about this spirit in advance:

> This know also, that in the last days perilous times shall come. For men shall be lovers of their own selves, covetous, boasters, proud, blasphemers, disobedient to parents, unthankful, unholy, without

natural affection, trucebreakers, false accusers, incontinent, fierce, despisers of those that are good, traitors, heady, high-minded, lovers of pleasures more than lovers of God; having a form of godliness, but denying the power thereof: from such turn away. (2 Tim. 3:1–5)

The Greek word translated "perilous" in verse 1 of this passage appears once more in the New Testament, in the account of the demonized man of Gadara who was extremely "fierce" or violent. As we consider Paul's prediction that the last days will be fierce and violent, consider this panoramic snapshot of our society today and how it has affected or infected the church:

1. Twenty-five percent of all women will be abused at some point during their lives.[1]

2. Some form of spousal abuse occurs in 30 to 50 percent of the marriages in America.[2]

3. Nearly five out of every ten pregnancies in the United States of America end in abortion. The same high-ranking leaders who maneuver or veto any bill that would put an end to partial-birth abortion can quote more scriptures than most preachers that I know.[3]

4. Evidence indicates that a demonic spirit of disease has been released in the earth that goes far beyond the usual patterns of human disease occurrence and epidemic growth. The bubonic plague, the scourge of Europe from 1348 to the 1600s, resurfaced in the twentieth century on the continent of Africa. Cholera and polio also struck the continent in epidemic proportions in 1999, and the HIV/AIDS epidemic swept through virtually every sector of society in Zimbabwe and other African nations.

5. A spirit of anger is plaguing our roadways. The National Highway Traffic Safety Administration (NHTSA) listed road rage as the number one traffic problem in America. The NHTSA didn't focus on the traditional problems of too few traffic lights or overpowered automobile engines. The problem is angry people who lose control of themselves and their cars. The U.S. Department of Transportation (DOT) reported that 250,000 people were killed on American highways between 1990 and 1996. According to the DOT, *two-thirds* of those fatalities, or almost 167,000 deaths, *were directly related to road rage.*[4]

6. A spirit of suicide is stalking the land. Teen suicide ranks as the second leading cause of death for those ages 15 to 19.[5] This is a standing indictment against the church of Jesus Christ! We have failed to introduce our children to the Prince of Peace and the Author of joy unspeakable and full of glory.

7. A spirit of perversion has joined forces with the spirit of violence to spawn a disgusting new class of brutal crimes against the human race.

8. A spirit of witchcraft, satanism, and the occult is using man's innate interest in the supernatural realm to gain entrance to human souls on an unprecedented scale. Familiar spirits, spirits of demons and witchcraft, and spirits of New Age deceit all flow freely through our media and the entertainment industry.

9. A spirit of pornography is gaining ground and "converts" at an astounding rate. One in five American adults has visited a sexually oriented Web site, according to a survey conducted by Zogby International for Focus on the Family. The poll

also revealed that 17.8 percent of born-again Christians have visited a sex site.[6] Seventy percent of pornographic magazines end up in the hands of *underage minors*.[7] Once such twisted images and the spirit behind them enter the human psyche, it takes the supernatural hand of God to cleanse the mind and free the human spirit of their grip.

10. A spirit of murder is casting its dark shadow over every square mile of our nation. Communities and demographic groups we believed would always be safe have been devastated by mass murders and unspeakable violence.

THE PROBLEM IS THAT WE NO LONGER CALL SIN "SIN"

I'm tired of hearing psychobabble delivered from our pulpits while big-name TV preachers do their best to corner the market on the Christian crowd with ear-tickling enticements and tantalizing fundraising offers. The problem is that we no longer call sin "sin."

Alcoholism is now a "disease," so state governments can benefit from sin on both ends of the "market." State governments spend multiplied millions of dollars a month promoting state-owned and state-operated liquor stores; and the same media outlets run promotions for state-run and state-sponsored alcoholism treatment and rehabilitation centers. When are we going to wake up?

Compulsive liars are no longer called sinners; they are merely "extroverts" with lively imaginations. Murderers are now "victims" of their tortured psychological pasts, and the true victims of their crimes are forgotten while their killers make the late-night talk show circuit. Adultery is no longer considered a sin in Hollywood (or in 90 percent of the church); it is the grist of prime-time ratings points and morning coffee breaks. "We serve the God of a second chance, don't we?" Yes, but some of us are running out of chances.

What happened to God's mandate that we grow up "unto the measure of the stature of the fullness of Christ" (Eph. 4:13)? Paul stated, "When I was a child, I spake as a child, I understood as a child, I thought as a child: but when I became a man, I put away childish things" (1 Cor. 13:11). How long will the church wait before she rises up in maturity and majesty to wield the power of God almighty Himself?

This may seem like old news now, but I visited Columbine High School in Colorado shortly after the massacre took place. I still have fresh memories of that old news. I can still see the blood splattered all over the ceilings, and tabletops so riddled by bullets they looked as if they'd been in a Beirut war zone. Shattered glass carpeted the hallways and classrooms, and the walls were stained by blood and smoke.

ARMED WITH A DERANGED PLAN TO MASSACRE THEIR CLASSMATES

Two young men armed with an automatic assault rifle, an assault pistol, two sawed-off 12-gauge shotguns, approximately sixty homemade bombs, and a deranged plan to massacre their class-mates caused the carnage. I stood at an entrance to the school and was met by a sharp-looking businessman whose beard had grown out a little. I noticed that his eyes looked hollow when he spoke to me, "Pastor Parsley, could I have an opportunity to look into your camera and talk to America?" When I nodded yes and asked who he was, he said, "I'm Rachel Scott's father. They made a shrine out of my daughter's car right over there."

Then Mr. Scott told me, "On Hitler's birthday, those two young men walked right past where we are standing now, Pastor Parsley.

Rachel was sitting right beside that little tree, eating her lunch and talking to one of her friends. They walked up to her and asked, 'Do you believe in God?' Rachel gave them a slight grin and said, 'Well, yes, why?' Then one of them pulled a 12-gauge shotgun from underneath his trench coat. My daughter was the first one slain, Pastor."

Mr. Scott looked into the Breakthrough Media Ministries television camera and said, "Here is what I want you to do, young people: defy any authority that violates your conscience, and stand in the middle of your hallway and pray! They can't put all of you out of school."

Afterward, he looked at me and said, "Pastor Parsley, do you see those blown-out windows up there? That's the library. Rachel, my daughter, was seventeen. My son was sixteen, and he was in the library when the gunmen came in. He said that God told him, 'Act like you are dead. Try to not even breathe.' The gunmen shot and killed the students lying on either side of him underneath that table.

"My son was the young man the CNN helicopter cameras showed leading people in prayer outside the school building while the blood of his friends dripped off his body and clothing," Mr. Scott said. "He didn't know until the following day that his own sister was the first one killed that day, or that her lifeless body was lying in the parking lot."

COLUMBINE GOT A REPRIEVE ON THE PRAYER BAN FOR ONE DAY

Prayer was banned in that upper-middle-class American high school until April 20, 1999. The students must have gotten a reprieve that day from the Supreme Court and the American Civil Liberties Union (ACLU).

I didn't sleep for three days after that demonic attack. It is likely that all Americans above the age of six will have the bloody images of the Columbine massacre burned into their memories for life. It symbolizes the senseless brutality and murder beginning to dominate our society.

I am not the kind of preacher who believes there is a demon under every rock—I usually don't give the devil and his realm a moment's thought. However, the apostle Paul said we should not be ignorant of Satan's devices. Lest we be ignorant, we need to open our spiritual eyes and understand that the devil is systematically executing our children and laughing at us as we stick our heads in the religious sand and sing, "This is the day that the Lord hath made." This is the day the Lord has made, but it is time for Christians to roll out of their spiritual beds and buckle up for battle. It's God's day, but our ignorance and apathy have let Satan have his way.

Did you know that eleven of the twelve children slain at Columbine High School were born-again, Bible-carrying Christians who faithfully attended prayer meetings and preached the gospel of Jesus Christ in their high school?[8] Why didn't CNN or one of the other major news networks report that? The news media also failed to report that every child killed at Paducah High School in Kentucky was a born-again, Spirit-filled disciple of Christ. This tightly focused epidemic of violence is neither an accident nor a coincidence. It reveals the existence of a demonic assignment in the heavenlies.

I THINK IT IS TIME TO RESPOND

Death is stalking our cities and the halls of our schools and shopping malls with hatred for a heart. Satan himself has released fiery darts against the saints from the smoke-filled, ink-black corridors of the doomed and the damned. The devil has made war with us. *I think it is time for us to respond.*

Even a casual review of the daily news provides evidence of a vast subsurface (spiritual) epidemic of anger, violence, and senseless mayhem sweeping through American society. It is not enough for us to shake our heads in disbelief or disapproval and say, "Woe is me. I wish I could do something about that. Gee, isn't that too bad?" It is time for us to run to the battle with the supernatural weapons of our warfare.

God's answer to perilous times is a glorious church filled with light and power. No matter how fierce or violent a demon spirit may be, it must bow its knee before the name of Jesus and the power of the living Christ in a strong believer. In the days to come, we must become people who do what Jesus said we would do! "These signs shall follow them that believe; *in my name shall they cast out devils*" (Mark 16:17, italics mine).

My pastor and spiritual father, the late Dr. Lester Sumrall, modeled this truth for us throughout most of his adult life. He was called to preach at the age of seventeen and ministered across America. Then he hooked up with a teacher from Britain named Howard Carter. Many believe that Howard Carter single-handedly restored the biblical revelation of the nine gifts of the Spirit to the body of Christ in the twentieth century.

In his twenty-first year, Dr. Sumrall ended up in Indonesia with Howard Carter. While Dr. Carter conducted teaching meetings in one place, Dr. Sumrall held evangelistic meetings at another location.

THE GIRL SLITHERED LIKE A SNAKE
BEFORE THE STUNNED CROWD

Dr. Sumrall described to me what happened after he took his seat on the platform. The large crowd filled the church building with beautiful singing. Suddenly a twelve-year-old girl began to slither across the floor like a serpent while undulating up and down with her arms stretched out behind her. Green foam came out of her nostrils and her mouth as she went back and forth before the stunned crowd. The serpentlike movements stopped only when the girl turned and looked at the preachers on the platform.

Dr. Sumrall said, "I looked at the pastor, and he was counting the lights. Then I looked for an usher, but they were all hidden behind some heavyset women. So I did the only thing an American evangelist knew to do—I began to pray: 'O God, save souls! Save souls, God! O God, save souls!'"

Then God replied, "I can't save souls because that thing down there is between you and the souls." Dr. Sumrall said, "I know! Why don't You do something about it?" God said, "I'm not going to do anything about it. *You* do something about it."

Dr. Sumrall said, "I didn't know what to do. I had been in a pentecostal denomination all my life, but we never heard sermons about demons. Nobody wanted to talk about demons back then." (Nobody wants to talk about demons today either.)

GET UP AND SIT DOWN!

He reached out with his hand to grasp the pulpit before offering the usual compliment about the beautiful scenery in the area, but according to Dr. Sumrall, "The minute I laid my hand on that pulpit something came up out of my belly. It didn't come out of my mind, or I would have never said it. Up out of my belly came the words, 'Get up and sit down!'" He said the young girl got up, wiped the green foam off her face, and sat down. She sat there and stared at him for forty-five minutes without moving.

"I preached my sermon and prepared to give the altar call," Dr. Sumrall said. "Then just as I was about to quote John 3:16, *it happened again*. Up out of my belly came the words, 'Come out of her!'" He said he had no idea what he had said, but he knows no one taught him those words. All of a sudden the girl's contorted face straightened out, and she began to talk to the person next to her. Dr. Sumrall ran down to where she was seated and asked his interpreter, "What is she saying?" The amazed interpreter said, "She's saying, 'Where am I? What am I doing here?'"

Dr. Sumrall said he was "glad to get out of that one," and he returned to his room and told Dr. Carter, "It was the craziest thing you've ever seen. I never want to get in a mess like that again." Dr. Carter said, "Well, it sounds to me like it turned out pretty good." Dr. Sumrall shook his head and said, "Well, you weren't there. It didn't happen to you."

Two nights later in Java, Dr. Sumrall walked into the service behind his interpreter who reached the platform ahead of him. As Dr. Sumrall passed through the side aisle, a woman suddenly grabbed his coat sleeve and said, "You have a little black angel in you, and I have a pretty white angel in me."

I SLAPPED MY RIGHT HAND ON HER LEFT JAW AND . . .

The interpreter urged Dr. Sumrall to come on up to the stage after he noticed the evangelist had stopped in the aisle. He told him, "I can't come; she's got me by the sleeve!" Dr. Sumrall described what happened next: "I threw down my briefcase and slapped my left hand on her right jaw and vice versa. Then I shouted as loud as I could, 'Come out of her!'"

(This is the way to set America free. Forget the religious programs and plans. Lay aside the powerless three-point sermon plus a poem you planned to deliver on Sunday. Don't bother to book the Nashville Gospel Has-Beens and the Holy Motown Wanna-Bes. You have to have something rise up supernaturally from within your spirit and shout in the authority of Christ Jesus, "Come out!")

The woman's eyes immediately refocused, and she said, "Oh, my gosh, what have I done?" Dr. Sumrall said, "Well, you grabbed hold of my coat, and I am trying to go preach." She said, "I do the craziest things. Fifteen years ago I got so angry at my husband that I asked a witch doctor to curse him. Instead I became cursed. For fifteen years I've been in this bondage."

That night Dr. Sumrall told Dr. Carter, "It happened again. I just want to be a nice American evangelist, and look at what is happening to me!" Dr. Carter said, "Well, it sounds like it turned out pretty good." Again Dr. Sumrall said, "Well, you weren't there. It didn't happen to you."

Two nights later, the man who drove Dr. Sumrall to his hotel after the service said, "Would you come and pray with my wife?" Dr. Sumrall said, "I suppose I will since you are the only one who knows the way to the hotel. I'd have to walk any other way."

The man drove them up to his beautiful home, and they walked inside. The moment they walked through the door, the man quickly shut the door and locked it. That was odd enough, but then Dr. Sumrall saw a naked woman crouched on top of a seven-foot-high wooden wardrobe. As the door lock clicked, she came sailing head-first off that wardrobe! If the man hadn't been strong, she would have broken her neck on the tile floor. He caught the woman in midair, quickly wrapped her in a sheet, and set her down in a chair. Then he turned to Dr. Sumrall and said, "This is my wife. Now cast it out of her." Dr. Sumrall dealt with the demon operating through this woman in the same way he dealt with other demons. He looked into the woman's eyes and spoke directly to the demon power within her, "Come out of her! In the name of Jesus, come out!" She was instantly set free from her bondage by the power of God.

IT CAME ON ME AGAIN!

Dr. Sumrall told me, "I was never so glad to get out of a place in my life! I left Asia and crossed Russia by rail on the Trans-Siberian

Express to reach Poland." At that point, he thought, *Surely I'll get away from that mess over here.* As he waited to preach in a beautiful church building in Poland, the congregation began to worship God in song when a woman on the front row started to sing and chant, "Hallelujah, hallelujah, hallelujah, hallelujah!"

Dr. Sumrall said, "It came on me again. I looked at that woman and said, 'Shut up!' I wished I had never said it. Instead of being set free, she suddenly shifted from saying 'Hallelujah' to barking like a dog!"

He thought, *Oh, dear God, it's in Europe too! Whatever Asian disorder those people had in Indonesia has moved over here to Europe.* He realized later that the problem wasn't a migrating spirit from hell. The Spirit of God within *him* was stirring up the devil in them.

(If you ever wonder why all kinds of crazy things seem to happen around you, it may well be that God puts you in situations and fills you full of the Holy Spirit and power. Perhaps God brought you to the kingdom for such a time as this!)

After Dr. Sumrall worked his way through that situation, he said, "I was really glad to get on a boat and head back across the Atlantic. I was raised in America, and I had never seen anything like that. I thought, *Once I get back home I'll be rid of this thing.*"

Dr. Sumrall was scheduled to preach in a church pastored by Dr. Houston, who was one of his elders. As it turned out, he preached the Sunday morning service for one of Dr. Houston's pastor friends instead, and he was scheduled to preach the evening service for Dr. Houston.

After that morning service, the host pastor asked him, "Would you go and pray for one of my saints?" Dr. Sumrall told me, "The man had just fed me a good beef dinner and I hated not to say yes, so I headed over there. When we arrived at the person's home, I walked into the craziest mess you ever saw in your life."

HE WAS SO CATATONIC THAT
HIS LIMBS FROZE IN ONE POSITION

When Dr. Sumrall walked through the door, he saw a man sitting on a wooden chair in the middle of the living room. He must have been twenty-five years old, but his mother was feeding him with a little spoon while begging her son, "Oh, darling, please speak to your mother. Speak to Mama. It has been six months since you said a word." Dr. Sumrall learned later that the man, who was raised in a Christian home, had been perfectly normal. The day of the visit, the man was so catatonic that if they lifted his arm away from his side, it froze into position for twenty-four hours. If they pointed his finger, the same thing happened. If they put him in bed, they found him in the exact position the next morning.

Most of the people familiar with his case thought he had lost his mind, but the truth is that the problems began after some of his church friends said, "Hey, have you ever watched a table lift off the ground? We have. In fact, we know how to do it." In the end, he decided to see for himself if his friends could levitate the table. He had no recollection of what happened after that.

His parents found him in the catatonic state the next morning. His shirt had been torn off, and blood was still oozing from deep gashes across his chest as if someone had clawed him. He lay bleeding there on the steps all night long. His parents brought him back into their home, but all they could do was keep him alive by feeding him like a baby day after day.

Dr. Sumrall said, "When I walked into the room, something hit me. I went running across that room, shouting as loud as I could, 'Speak to your mother; and come out of him, you foul devil!' Immediately the man became as normal as he had ever been."

These kinds of experiences occurred throughout Dr. Sumrall's decades of ministry, leading his critics to label him a "devil chaser."

The truth is that the power of God within the man rocked the kingdom of darkness wherever he went. Would to God we could all qualify for that label, devil chaser. It seems to me that is what God expects of *all of us,* powerless critics included.

WE NEED MORE GOD-ORDAINED DEVIL CHASERS

Have you ever wondered what makes people do the crazy and illogical things they do? What on earth would make our teenagers smoke marijuana after they've tasted the things of God? What on earth would make a preacher climb into bed with a rouge-streaked, blurry-eyed floozy and forfeit his family and lifetime of ministry? I'll tell you what it is: it is a demon. All of us will be held accountable for our choices and our sins, but we need to recognize that a malignant outside force is working overtime to tempt, try, and destroy us. I think it is about time for more God-ordained devil chasers to come on the scene, don't you?

It was my privilege to serve and learn from Dr. Lester Sumrall for most of my adult ministry, and I've asked the Lord for the same anointing He placed on Dr. Sumrall's life. Recently the Lord promised to set free ten thousand homosexuals by television in one mighty blast of anointing as I shout in the Holy Spirit of power, "Come out!"

I believe it will come to pass, even if the politically correct take away my ministry and rip the microphone out of my hands. It doesn't matter. This battle is in the spirit, not the flesh. If I have to, I'll cup my hands and shout, "Come out!" at the top of my lungs. America needs to be set free from the grip of demon power, and it will come about only through the delivering power of God.

We are talking about dealing with the spirit of the age. The Bible says, "As it was in the days of Noah, so shall it be also in the days of the Son of man" (Luke 17:26). Violence filled the land in Noah's day, and it is doing the same thing in our day. By the time American children turn eighteen, they have seen an average of 200,000 acts of violence on television alone, including 25,000 cold-blooded murders.[9]

Our children are exposed to these video game advertisements: "More fun than shooting your neighbor's cat," "Kill your friends guilt free," and "Get in touch with your gun-toting cold-blooded murdering self."[10]

Meanwhile we gather on Sunday morning to sing, "This is the day the Lord hath made." According to one survey, the rest of the time many of us watch R-rated movies just as often as those who claim no experience with Jesus Christ![11]

"I AWAKEN A COLLECTIVE DISBELIEF IN CHRISTIANITY"

One singer-performer who has been popular with American teens is Marilyn Manson. He created his stage name by joining the first name of a late Hollywood sex goddess with the second name of a demonic cult murderer named Charles Manson. Wearing nothing but a black G-string, this man straps himself to a wooden cross for his outrageous concerts. Marilyn Manson openly declares, "My role is to awaken a collective disbelief in Christianity and its God."[12]

Song lyrics come and go, but there is no mistaking the timeless spirit behind them. The song "Country Death Song" crooned to our children,

> I started making plans to kill my own,
> come little daughter we'll have some fun.
> I led her to a hole,
> I gave her a push,
> I threw my own child into a bottomless pit.

Another "classic" entitled "Misery Machine" declared, "Careen down highway 666, I'm fueled by filth and fury."

In that context, consider the words of the parents who say, "I don't understand why Johnny treats me with such disrespect. What does he have in his room? I don't know. I don't want to invade his privacy." There's a difference between privacy and secrecy. (You need privacy to go to the bathroom and take a bath, and that's it.)

God goes beyond the outward appearances in our lives to discern our heart motivation. We need to do the same thing with our children and with one another. Whom do you want to be like? What do you want to represent? The Bible urges us to glorify God with our bodies. God is also concerned about our associations. You prove your allegiance by the way you dress and the attitudes you display.

SIN DULLS YOUR DEEP DESIRE FOR TRULY SPIRITUAL THINGS

As a child, John Wesley asked, "Mother, what is sin?" She replied, "John, sin is anything that impedes the tenderness of your conscience, weakens your reasoning, or dulls your deep desire for truly spiritual things. John, sin is anything that exalts the authority of your body and your mind above your spirit."

Let me plead with you: shun the wrong; do the right. Walk in your teenager's bedroom and say, "Now, darling, I love you and let me tell you why this will destroy you. Let me warn you." Find something that's anointed. Find somebody who can get you into the presence of God. If you can't get in there and make a joyful noise, just get into the presence of God. Shut yourself away, and when you come out of there, I'll tell you what will happen: you'll be so full of the glory of God that men and women are gonna fall down in front of you and say, "My God, you convict me of my sin by the very presence of God that rests upon you."

If we say we have no sin, we deceive ourselves. Examine yourself and the atmosphere of your home. The power of God can fix right now anything that is wrong at your house. The living God revealed in the remnant church can fix anything wrong in America!

If you are free, then act like it! If you are not free, then get free! The spirit of the age scores its greatest victory when the blood-bought people of God give blind allegiance to corrupt spiritual and political leadership.

"Well, my family has always voted Democratic . . . I've always voted the Republican Party line." This blind allegiance to the flawed institutions of man must stop. No matter who the leader is (including the skin color or gender), and regardless of the political party or affiliation he claims to embrace, we must say with one mind and in one accord: "We refuse to yoke up with you *if you do not adhere to the concepts and the precepts of God's Word.*"

LET GOD'S WORD BE YOUR FOUNDATION

You and I have been given *authority* over the fallen god of this world. Now is the time to use that authority. Let God's Word be the foundation of your holy commission as a devil chaser and ambassador of the most high God:

> [He] *gave them power and authority over all devils,* and to cure diseases. (Luke 9:1, italics mine)

> Behold, *I give unto you power* to tread on serpents and scorpions, and *over all the power of the enemy:* and nothing [that means nothing, nothing, nothing, nothing, nothing, nothing, nothing, nothing, nothing] shall by any means hurt you. (Luke 10:19, italics mine)

Now is the judgment of this world: *now shall the prince of this world be cast out.* And I, if I be lifted up from the earth, will draw all men unto me. (John 12:31–32, italics mine)

The prince of this world is judged. (John 16:11, italics mine)

Jesus answered, My kingdom is *not of this world.* (John 18:36, italics mine)

What is the *exceeding greatness of his power to us-ward who believe,* according to the working of his mighty power, which he wrought in Christ, when he raised him from the dead, and set him at his own right hand in the heavenly places, *far above all principality, and power, and might, and dominion,* and every name that is named, not only in this world, but also in that which is to come. (Eph. 1:19–21, italics mine)

To the intent that now *unto the principalities and powers in heavenly places* might be known *by the church* the manifold wisdom of God, *according to the eternal purpose* which he purposed in Christ Jesus our Lord. (Eph. 3:10–11, italics mine)

For we wrestle not against flesh and blood, but against principalities, against powers, against the rulers of the darkness of this world, *against spiritual wickedness in high places.* Wherefore take unto you the whole armor of God, that ye may be able to withstand in the evil day, and having done all, to stand. (Eph. 6:12–13, italics mine)

For this purpose the Son of God was manifested, *that he might destroy the works of the devil.* (1 John 3:8, italics mine)

Finally consider Paul's warning from the Scriptures: "Neither *give place* to the devil" (Eph. 4:27, italics mine). That means you must give him "no position of opportunity." When it says not to give the devil "place," the Greek terms mean we must not give him any "space *limited by occupancy.*"

Do you want to know how to run the devil out of your life? Are you tired of Satan's occupation with your mind, your body, your friends, your family, and your public school? *Limit his space by occupancy.* Do what the Bible says: "Be not drunk with wine, wherein is excess; but *be filled with the Spirit*" (Eph. 5:18, italics mine). Pray this prayer with me before we go any farther:

> Father, let an anointing come upon us now such as we have never experienced in our lives. Make us vessels unto honor. Fill us with Your Holy Spirit, and send us forth as champions in Your harvest field. In Your name, we will defeat the spirit of the age in the power of the Holy Spirit. Together we shout, "Even so, come quickly, Lord Jesus!"

Now it is time to start a revolution.

CHAPTER 4

LET THE
REVOLUTION BEGIN

Time is literally pregnant to give birth to a
revolutionary people.

You should know this from the start: I came to start a revolution. Throughout the ages, countries and kingdoms have been birthed on the battlefield of a revolutionary movement. The crusades have always been championed by soldiers and citizens alike who refused to be denied, delayed, or deterred in their pursuit of a cause they believed to be deserving even of death itself.

There comes a time when negotiations have failed and talk is no longer tolerated. When we reach that point on the cosmic scale, all of creation begins to groan under the pressure of giving birth to a revolutionary movement.

When comfort and contentment no longer pacify the people, the cry "Freedom at any cost!" becomes the catalyst for revolutionary confrontation and change. The force driving this dynamic transition can trigger a genuine culture-shaking revival that changes the moral climate of entire cities. Its effect is felt like shock waves throughout the nation.

The early church was spawned during this kind of culture-shaking revival. Every man and woman who joined the early church—especially in Jerusalem—fully expected to die as martyrs for their faith. (What would that do to the attendance levels for the average "New Believers" class today?) At the very least, first-century converts knew they would be targeted for vicious social ostracism as misfits. The religious elitists mocked them, and their peers often shunned them in the marketplace and on the street.

THE FIERY PASSION OF THE EARLY SAINTS IS BURNING TODAY

Nevertheless, the early saints of the church were like Shadrach, Meshach, and Abednego of the Old Testament: *they would not bow!* I see the same fiery passion and determination beginning to burn today. A glorious church is rising out of the benign blur of indistinctness. I perceive a remnant people who will gladly lose their lives *for a cause they believe to be greater than themselves.*

A genuine culture-shaking revival will literally change the moral fiber of our cities, but I must caution you that this revolution is not for the timid. God is looking for people who have stepped over the line and out of their comfort zone at the sound of His call to their hearts. He will send only true disciples of Jesus Christ into the battle. You can recognize them by their lack of appetite for public position and popularity. They don't seek the privileges of position or a reassuring pat on the back. They are just happy to be in the battle.

WE MUST TAKE THE BLESSED HOPE TO THE HOPELESS

It is time for us to take up our weapons and invade the smoke-filled corridors of the doomed and the damned. We are called and anointed to grapple with the enemy for the souls of the depraved as well as the destitute. The King's orders are clear: take the blessed hope of the gospel to hopeless humanity; engage your archenemy, Satan, to set your hell-bound generation free.

We must thrust the sickle of God into our society and reap souls as never before because the harvest truly is ripe. God is looking for a remnant people to stand in the gap and make up the hedge for humanity. He requires warriors who don't have to be right or recognized, rewarded or regarded.

Sound the alarm: heaven has launched a Holy Spirit invasion! *Let the revolution begin.*

The critics complain that our army doesn't look like much right now. They are right. In the spirit realm, we probably look like Gomer Pyle's infantry platoon, but little is much when God is in it. The Lord managed to turn the world upside down two thousand years ago using another band of twelve misfits from nowhere. What will He accomplish with us?

Isaiah the prophet spoke of a remnant band who dared to go into no-man's-land and rebuild the "old waste places." Remember what he said: "They that shall be of thee shall build the old waste places: thou shalt raise up the foundations of many generations; and thou shalt be called, The repairer of the breach, The restorer of paths to dwell in" (Isa. 58:12). The die has been cast. It is too late to turn back now. The remnant on the brink has been launched into the desolate places of darkness like an arrow of light in flight.

Few people want to leave the comfort of their padded pews, air-conditioned sanctuaries, and low-commitment church routines to actually do the work of the ministry where it is needed the most. That's all right; God has always had a remnant reserved for His purposes.

We don't understand that we have entered another period I call the "fullness of time." In our day, Father God has gone into Mother Time to give birth to the child of His old age. The child of the

Ancient of Day's "old age" is always the delivering child. Abraham's Isaac was the delivering child. Jesse's son, David, the child of his old age, was the deliverer of Israel. Time is literally pregnant to give birth to a revolutionary people.

God is sending us in the fullness of time to recover and rebuild the ravaged ruins of human lives left desolate by Satan's hatred. He has anointed us to cleanse and revive those inhabited and controlled by demon spirits. We are dispatched to "raise up the foundations of many generations," and we are called "the repairers of the breach" and "the restorers of paths to dwell in."

I am encouraged as I write these words. God's passionate remnant is stirring again. A church is rising up within the worldwide church, a remnant church if you will. Every local church has its professional pew sitters and religious churchgoers who are content to remain "in the way" all of their lives. God loves them, but He knows He can't count on them when it is time to charge hell's gates.

The remnant people, however, are a different breed. Something about them sets them apart. Somehow you get the feeling they were born to do great exploits for God. Every pastor prays for more remnant folks because he can build the kingdom of God with those people.

God has always had a remnant, a people within a people. He usually sets apart at least one individual in a family for some extra turns on the Potter's wheel. He tends to spend more time preparing, making, breaking, and remaking these people to form special vessels of healing and deliverance. He likes to pour divine power into these tried and proved vessels, but only after they go through the tempering fires of testing to make them strong.

Remnant people have another quality that sets them apart from the rest: they exhibit a tremendous dissatisfaction with the status quo when God has been displaced from first place in any way. They have little patience for conducting church as usual if it involves preserving a "form of godliness, but denying the power thereof" (2 Tim. 3:5).

WHAT DO YOU LOVE THE MOST?

The members of this remnant band are not satisfied with a few choir songs that tickle the emotions, followed by a feel-good message tailored to please an impatient congregation. They probe below the surface to see what is loved the most. They can sense when something is missing, even when everything else looks right.

Jesus said, "Salt is good: but if the salt have lost his saltness, wherewith will ye season it? Have salt in yourselves, and have peace one with another" (Mark 9:50). In another place, He put the responsibility squarely on our shoulders when He said, "Ye are the salt of the earth: but if the salt have lost his savour, wherewith shall it be salted? it is thenceforth good for nothing, but to be cast out, and to be trodden under foot of men" (Matt. 5:13).

When God sends out His remnant people as vessels containing His divine mix of power, conviction, grace, and mercy, the anointing they deliver can easily trigger a revolution. God's revolutions bring divine change to all of mankind. That was precisely what Jesus did with the twelve disciples and one hardheaded, reluctant recruit taken from Gamaliel's rabbinic seminary (Saul who was known as Paul).

Jesus constantly talked about different kinds of vessels. He told the disciples, "Neither do men put new wine into old bottles: else the bottles break, and the wine runneth out, and the bottles perish: but they put new wine into new bottles, and both are preserved" (Matt. 9:17).

CAN YOU ACCOMMODATE THE PRESSURES OF CHANGE?

When God's fresh move of the Spirit comes in—the new wine—the old wineskins (*bottles* in KJV) that refused to be changed will not be

ready to receive from God. Jesus wasn't talking about the chronological age of sheepskin wine containers; He was referring to us and
our ability to endure and accommodate the pressures of *change*. If
we try to force or fit His gift into old wineskins, they will burst, and
we will lose both the new wine and the older vessels.

Brittle and stiff vessels are unable to receive a fresh move or hear
a fresh word from God. They are too satisfied with what they had
once upon a time to adjust their spiritual sails to catch the winds of
God. They would rather anchor themselves to their church pew and
say, "It doesn't feel as if the wind is blowing in here anymore."

The truth is that God is pouring out brand-new wine right now.
According to the testimony of three gospel accounts, Jesus said new
wine could be put only in *new bottles*. (See Matt. 9:17; Mark 2:22;
Luke 5:37–38.) Are you ready to shed your "old wineskin" so you
can become a vessel equipped to carry His presence?

DESPITE THE HYPE, SOMETHING *IS* COMING!

Isolated pockets of revival are springing up in various locations
around the United States and the world. Unfortunately shadows are
being substituted for substance, pockets of revival are called a flood,
and trickles are called a river. Despite the hype, something *is* coming!

At times, the runoff of one local overflow joins with that of
another, and a little river of God's glory can be seen. I have to tell
you that I'm convinced this amounts to a few sprinkles before the
deluge of His glory hits this planet.

The river is about to become an ocean, and the ocean is about
to overflow beyond its established shores. God is about to send a
Holy Spirit revival in which the reapers are going to overtake the
sowers. The harvest will run to the reapers before the sowers can get
their seed in the ground.

God is going to send the "former rain" and the "latter rain" together in one great downpour. When this thing comes in full force, the transformation in your life will be so great that you won't recognize yourself. You are going to walk up and spit in the eye of the devil instead of trembling underneath your dinner table.

GOD IS PREPARING VESSELS FOR REVIVAL

You are about to eat and drink some things in the Spirit that you've never had before. You are about to feel something you've never felt because God is preparing the *vessels of revival* for a revolution.

Something is coming.

Why get a new wineskin? Why didn't He just say, "Bring Me a handful of salt"? He said something specific. He didn't say, "Just bring Me some salt." We know what salt is for: preservation, restoration, prominence. It represents the eternal, the infallible, the "unfailable." He didn't just say, "Bring Me a handful of salt" (or "Ye are the salt of the earth"). He also said, "Bring me a *new* wineskin." Why? God is preparing a vessel pure enough, flexible enough, strong enough, and bold enough to contain His revolutionary, life-transforming, kingdom-overturning glory.

It should be obvious that no ordinary old vessel will do. Have you ever wondered why the Bible says, "But we all, with open face beholding as in a glass the glory of the Lord, are changed into the same image from glory to glory, even as by the Spirit of the Lord" (2 Cor. 3:18)?

VESSELS MUST BE READY TO CARRY HIS GLORY

He is changing (*metamorphosing*) us into His image from glory to glory so He can pour His glory over the earth. He has to have vessels ready and waiting to catch it, carry it, and pour it out to the world.

(God has always used people on earth to do His work among people.)

The great harvest is coming, and God is moving on His remnant people at times when everyone else is asleep. We find ourselves awakened from a sound sleep with a moan rising from our hearts: "O God, as the deer panteth for the water brooks, so my soul longeth after Thee, O Lord."

We walk through the earth with a grand distraction; we have a holy mission that consumes our waking hours. Our eyes are fixed on the prize of the mark of the high calling of God in Christ. We find ourselves saying, "I'm not getting involved in your pettiness. Don't you sense that God is about to do something?"

The misconception of the church is that the wineskin itself is the cure. The wineskin is only what *contains* the cure. The church thought *it* was the cure, and it labored to produce nothing more than numerical growth.

The national newsmagazines may poll five hundred people by telephone and declare the following week, "America Returns to Church," but we shouldn't be as concerned about people going back to church as we are about *what they will receive* when they get there.

WE NOTICED SOMETHING WAS MISSING WHEN DARKNESS BEGAN TO FALL

There is a stirring in the air. We are like the woman in Jesus' parable who lost a valuable coin (Luke 15:8). We never thought about it much until we suddenly noticed the shadows of darkness beginning to fall. Then we said, "Wait a minute. It seems that we're missing something here!"

Something happens within you when darkness sets in all around you. You feel a change coming on when pressures beset you, when the local newspaper prints a negative article about you, or when you get a bad report from the doctor. You start looking for something you lost when your friends forsake you without warning. You say, "Wait a minute. Do I have everything I need to make it through the darkness to the dawn?"

The woman in the parable said, "I've got to find my coin," and she grabbed a broom and started sweeping.

A DIVINE DISCOMFORT FILLS OUR SOULS

There is a stirring in our hearts. We have a sense of uneasiness, and a divine discomfort fills our souls. Everything looks right, but we are missing something. People don't understand because we have attractive buildings, property, transportation departments, money, television and radio programs, printed pieces, mailing lists, and enough plans and programs to last the millennium. We have Little League teams, middle league teams, in-between league teams, adult sports, singles groups, married groups, divorced groups, spaghetti dinners, and the tastiest rib fests in town! What more could we ask for?

Some of us have to tell the truth: "We don't have what we want. We're *missing something*." I want God to flow out of my life so powerfully that when my shadow passes over the sick, they are instantly healed. It isn't happening yet. I want the presence of God to wear me like a suit. If a poisonous serpent is foolish enough to bite me in the performance of my God-given duties, I'll shake it off and go about the ministry. I want victory and joy unspeakable and full of glory.

The church has traded the banners of doctrine for self-help, prosperity, and success seminars until it resembles a multilevel marketing organization more than a New Testament church. Christianity is looking and acting more like a man-centered cult and less like a spiritual organism and the body of Christ. We have a form of godliness, but we deny its power.

THE CHURCH IS TO BE A VEHICLE OF CHANGE

There's something missing: the church doesn't know its purpose anymore. The church was planted on the earth to be a vehicle of change. We are here to destroy the works of the devil and bring the glory of God to this hell-bound generation. Even the prayer Jesus taught us cries out to our heavenly Father, "Thy kingdom come. Thy will be done *in earth,* as it is in heaven" (Matt. 6:10, italics mine).

Do you know what is missing? It is the resurrection life of Christ. Your Bible says this about Jesus: "In him was life; and the life was the light of men. And the light shineth in darkness; and the darkness comprehended it not" (John 1:4–5). Light showed up everywhere Jesus went. When He walked onto the seashore at Gadara, two thousand demons paused in the act of tormenting their helpless human host to bow before Jesus and cry out, "What have I to do with thee, Jesus, thou Son of the most high God? I adjure thee by God, that thou torment me not" (Mark 5:7).

CREATURES OF DARKNESS SCATTERED AND WINESKINS BEGAN TO BURST

The demons called Legion begged the King of glory to "turn the light out"! When Jesus showed up, the creatures of darkness scattered, and old wineskins began to burst.

The New Testament church in the book of Acts had what I'm talking about—the members had resurrection life and a healthy awe of the living God. People who lied to the Holy Spirit were known to drop dead right in front of their preachers. They also saw dead folks raised to life, and their leaders freed from jail cells through earthquakes and angelic intervention.

Try to find Jesus in most modern church services, but be prepared for disappointment. Too many Christians treat their favorite leaders like Christian gurus because of the thrill they feel when they are slain in the Spirit or experience some other manifestation. I believe in the power of the Holy Spirit, but I'm sick of idol worship in the church! It's time to lay aside our fleshly idols and seek the One who saved us. No one else shed his blood for us, so no one else deserves the credit or the glory.

Search the book of Acts and show me one place where any appeal was made to get unsaved people into any form of church service. It didn't happen because it wasn't needed.

BRING YOUR BIBLE (BUT FORGET THE EGG TIMER)

The modern church has done everything conceivable to coax its prayerless saints back into the prayer closet. Popular prayer training programs encourage believers to approach prayer with their Bibles and an egg timer. I assume that as many Christians used the timers to "count the painful minutes" as used them to make sure they "put in their time."

I applaud the noble motives behind the many prayer courses used by churches across the nation. Christians must pray, or they will fail in their walk with Christ. Even the Son of God felt the need to pray fervently, deeply, and often. Sometimes He prayed through the night and then ministered to the masses all the next day. Nevertheless, I have to say that our incorporation of a timer of any kind speaks volumes about our erroneous ideas concerning prayer.

Not once did the apostles pass out prayer cards and an egg timer to get the New Testament church into a prayer meeting. They didn't have praise seminars either. People who know what it means to be translated out of darkness and into God's marvelous light already know how to praise Him! They don't need a Hammond B-3 organ or a worship leader. They praise God all the time.

Show me, then I'll believe. Until then I'm looking for something that is *missing*. The Bible recorded that Jesus "must needs go through Samaria" (John 4:4). He was on a mission from God, and a divine appointment awaited Him with a lost woman of Samaria at Jacob's well. He didn't say He'd preach for a good salary; He just had to go. Understanding this story has helped me deal with the fire God placed within me recently.

I told my wife, Joni, "Honey, I wake up in the middle of the night almost every night. I have to keep paper and pencils and Bibles by my bed constantly, and I just can't sleep. Sometimes I beg God to let morning come, and I often walk through the house all night. I have to pour this out; it's burning within me. I can say with the prophet, there is 'fire shut up in my bones.' I don't have time to argue or negotiate with God. I simply have to go."

CALL ME POSSESSED, HELPLESS, AND HAPPY

I am possessed by the Spirit of God, and I can't help it; I have to go. I have to pray. I have to preach. I have to sing and shout and boldly witness to the lost. I "must needs go." A burning light is within me and I can't stop (and I wouldn't stop if I could—serving God on the brink is the most exciting lifestyle anyone could ever have)!

The newborn church in the book of Acts "ceased not to teach and preach Jesus Christ" (Acts 5:42). They didn't preach a method, a plan, or a program. They preached Jesus.

I have read and reread the fourth chapter of Luke all of my life, but only recently did I perceive what Jesus did after He read from the book of the prophet in the synagogue:

> The Spirit of the Lord is upon me, because he hath anointed me to preach the gospel to the poor; he hath sent me to heal the bro-ken-hearted, to preach deliverance to the captives, and recovering of sight to the blind, to set at liberty them that are bruised, to

preach the acceptable year of the Lord. *And he closed the book,* and he gave it again to the minister, and sat down. And the eyes of all them that were in the synagogue were fastened on him. And he began to say unto them, This day is this scripture fulfilled in your ears. (Luke 4:18–21, italics mine)

Jesus closed the book when He had become successful at revealing God's love to His creation. God is preparing a body to do nothing but *give expression* to the divine life He has placed within it.

THIS IS A MATTER OF DIVINE REVELATION AND REVOLUTION

This isn't about religion or a prayer meeting; it is about God's plan to reveal Himself to our lost and dying generation through His remnant church. It is about a revolution of the spirit realm affecting the natural realm on earth.

The Lord will go to great lengths to prepare His vessels for the infilling of His glory. Jesus went out of His way to intercept two dejected disciples on the road to Emmaus. He ended up walking with them for seven and a half miles before they stopped to eat. He didn't leave them until He had revealed Himself to them and set their hearts on fire! (See Luke 24:30–32.) It isn't any different with you. He won't let you go until He has revealed Himself to you and set your life on fire.

CHAPTER 5

HUNGER AND DESIRE
FUEL THE FIRE
OF REVOLUTION

God is searching among the slumbering saints for a few good candidates, a remnant of believers who will stand up in the spirit of Moses, point their fingers at Pharaoh, and shout, "Let God's people go!"

His search has revealed that something is missing in the American church, much as it was missing from five of the seven churches He addressed in the book of Revelation.[1] God's strategy to revive His sleeping bride and revolutionize the world requires revolutionary remnant people who are irrevocably marked by four characteristics that can't be missed.

I first heard the early beginnings of three of these characteristics after a friend sent me a ministry tape by an unnamed preacher entitled "Not Giving Up." I am indebted to this unknown preacher for triggering what has turned into a continuous search for understanding in what I now feel are four characteristics of revolutionary remnant people. They are (1) compelled by an inward desire, (2) to serve an infallible Leader, (3) through irresistible power, (4) based on absolute truth.

Men and women of such spiritual stock will not cave in under pressure. They are ideal weapons in the hand of God to launch world-changing revolution. The problem is that without the first component—*inward desire*—heaven's earthly invasion force will never make it out of boot camp!

Samuel the prophet faced a similar problem in his day. The people of Israel chose to forget the God of miracles who instructed Joshua to lead their forefathers across the river Jordan because they found the local fertility gods more to their liking. Samuel boldly confronted the sins and distractions of Israel and brought the people back into alignment with God's purposes.

He told the Israelites that they were guilty of crimes and misdemeanors against God because *they had departed from their convictions and godly traditions* to bow before forbidden gods. He required them to *identify their sin* and *repent*. And he pronounced a *blessing* upon their obedience (1 Sam. 7:3–6).

Samuel's influence changed the nation because it carried the force of absolute moral truth, and his life demonstrated his conviction and backed his language. Yet even Samuel was entangled in the quagmire of "generational degeneration" when his sons failed to walk with God as he did.

INWARD DESIRE IS THE FIRST COMPONENT
OF REVOLUTION

That brings us back to the first component of revival and revolution, inward desire. Apathy and indifference are two of the greatest obstacles to revival. John recorded in his gospel that Jesus said, "*Say not* ye, There are yet four months, and then cometh harvest? behold, I say unto you, Lift up your eyes, and look on the fields; for they are white already to harvest" (John 4:35, italics mine).

The New Testament church was in its third generation when John the elder statesman sat down to commit his gospel record to writing (as well as his Pastoral Epistles and the apocalyptic revelation).

The synoptic Gospels of Matthew, Mark, and Luke had been penned long ago, and John was already an old man when he wrote his gospel. His brother James was dead, and fiery Peter was gone too. The apostle Paul was executed in A.D. 68 in Rome's Mamertine Dungeon the same year Nero committed suicide,[2] a number of years before the church's hundred-year anniversary. Jerusalem had been leveled, and the Christians were spread across the expanse of the known world.

By that time, John had been boiled in oil three times and refused to die. He endured and outlived the persecution of Nero, and he was ultimately exiled to the island of Patmos, fifty miles off the coast of Ephesus, accompanied only by wild beasts.

Near the end of John's life, Roman emperor Domitian (Titus Flavius Domitianus), the fifth successor after Nero, encouraged the persecution of Christians and demanded that all men worship him, saying, "*Dominus et Deus*" ("Lord and God").[3] Meanwhile, John the Beloved heard a "great voice, as of a trumpet" say to him on the Lord's Day, "Write the things which thou hast seen, and the things which are, and the things which shall be hereafter" (Rev. 1:19).

THE SEEDS OF APOSTASY CAME TO FULL GROWTH

Apostasy was sown like seeds of leaven in the early years of the church. Those seeds came to full growth in the heresy of Gnosticism. The belief that flesh or matter is totally evil and spirit is the ultimate good invaded the church and threatened to mutate Christianity into something unrecognizable.

The Gnostics propagated the lie that Christ never came in the flesh, and that salvation can come only through secret knowledge of the spirit realm reserved (predictably) for a small, elite group of people. In other words, it set aside salvation by faith and took its converts right back into an impossible salvation-by-works scheme of man.

Thus, John did not write to the infant church; he wrote to an infirm third-generation church, a sick and weakened church in imminent danger of judgment. He set forth his gospel to replace that "missing something" and reattach the body to its Head.

John wrote with a sense of urgency because he sensed *something was wrong in the heart and the soul of the church,* and things had to change before it was eternally too late. The church had been battered by the deadening blows of the God haters and the naysayers.

Emperor Claudius drove many Christians out of Rome, and Nero completed the job by blaming them for setting the imperial city on fire. His successors in Rome, Vitellius and Vespasian, reduced Jerusalem to rubble and continued to persecute the church. Yet its greatest danger lurked within the church itself: the spirits of heresy, subversion, sedition, hedonism, and division.

In this disjointed and distressed time John the elder quoted the command of Jesus: "*Say not* ye, There are yet four months, and then cometh harvest?" (John 4:35, italics mine).

According to the "Rod Parsley translation," "Say not ye" means "Shut up! Hush! There is too much talking and not enough listening going on! There are too many voices. It is hard to distinguish the truth." The church had failed to heed the apostle Paul's warnings. The people were tossed about by "every wind of doctrine" and carried away by the lies of deceitful men (Eph. 4:14; 2 Tim. 3:4–7).

EACH GENERATION APPROACHES
TRUTH DIFFERENTLY

John wrote his gospel for the third generation of Christians, and that is of particular importance to us today because *we are the third American church generation* since God reintroduced the gifts and operations of the Holy Spirit in the Azusa Street visitations (1906–1908). Each generation seems to approach the original truth received in different ways.

In the first generation, truth becomes a conviction. When you first receive a truth, it becomes a conviction of passion that burns in your heart. This is especially true when personal experience verifies your conviction. Men will gladly lay down their lives for their convictions, but they will give you no opportunity to discuss compromise.

The second generation approaches the hard-won truths of the previous generation with cooler hearts. Secondhand truths without personal experience rarely remain convictions. They degenerate to mere persuasion. If I can persuade you to believe a thing, someone else can persuade you to disbelieve it. Conviction stands on the unwavering foundation of passion, but belief is left to wobble on the unsure foundation of persuasion. Persuasion goes only as far as the head, but conviction pierces to the very heart of man. Few men are willing to die for a mere belief.

People from the second generation are quick to discuss or debate the truth because after all, "It is only a belief, and beliefs can change." The moment the door to compromise begins to crack open, we reduce the church to an employment agency for people seeking self-advancement through their skills of persuasion and entertainment. In an era of second-generation believers, the arguments of men can quickly displace the revelation of God on the center stage of men. This is the sporting ground of heresy, schism, and ultimate damnation.

A CHURCH WITHOUT POWER RISES AND FALLS AT THE WHIMS OF MEN

Without the passion of conviction, the church loses its divine dynamic. *It is no longer a revolutionary force of dynamic change in the hearts and lives of human persons.* A church without power is nothing more than an institution, doomed to rise and fall with the changing fortunes and whims of men.

God had something better in mind when He sent His only begotten Son to hang between heaven and earth for the sins of man! Would He submit His Son to the unspeakable horror of the Cross merely to preserve the First Church of Superior Persuasion? God forbid.

When God almighty plucked His Son out of death's grasp and raised Him from the dead, He saw a glorious church founded and rooted in the revelation of His Son, not a monument to man's instability. He took 120 people energized by the power and passion of the Holy Spirit and evangelized the world in less than twenty years—without the benefit of a single television network, radio transmitter, printing press, or mailing list. No matter how you look at it, the fickle force of belief or mere mental persuasion could never power such an enterprise. This unequaled miracle could spring forth only from the fiery critical mass of passionate conviction.

The third generation tends to view its grandparents' truth as nothing more than an opinion. You know about opinions, don't you? Everybody has one. We have so eroded the foundation of truth in many of our churches that there is nothing left to stand on except the slippery slope of man's ever-changing opinion.

NEVER BOW DOWN TO THE SHRINE OF GOSPEL ENTERTAINMENT

Christians become spineless when there is no anointed preaching, doctrine, or Bible teaching in their local church. Their condition gets worse when they bow down at the shrine of gospel entertainment and base their opinion of the week on the latest statements of the gospel preaching stars. We can gain much from anointed preaching on television as long as we remember the only star worthy of worship in God's universe is the Bright and Morning Star, the risen Christ. We won't go wrong making *His* Word our truth for eternity. We also grow weak when we lose the hunger and desire that feed the fires of passion.

I'll never forget my first camp meeting.[4] About twelve of us piled into a motor home in Columbus, Ohio, and drove straight through to Houston, Texas. We didn't have a bathroom or a hotel room. We stopped at a gas station and took an "evangelist's bath" in the sink of the station's rest room. That tells you how hungry we were for God's Word.

The late Brother John Osteen's Oasis of Love conducted the meetings in its old metal building, and everyone sat on hard folding chairs. Brother Osteen let us bring food and drinks into the make-shift sanctuary back then, so somebody would run outside and bring back hot dogs while the rest of us held the seats.

I heard things in those meetings that I had never heard in my life. I was so hungry that I sat on that old hard folding chair from one service to the next without leaving. (I pray that we all get hungry for God again!) It didn't matter who picked up the microphone, we wanted to hear one more word from God. I sat there all week, and most of the time I felt as if my tail bone had been pushed up between my shoulder blades. Despite being bruised, sleepless, and sore, I wanted more of God.

CONSUMMATION ALWAYS LAUNCHES AN INITIATION

We are the third generation, and the good news is that the third generation is also known for new beginnings, completion, and consummation. God never brings anything to a close for any reason other than to build a platform. He never brings something to consummation for any reason other than to launch an initiation.

It is exciting to live right in the middle of God's divine preparation for a revolution. I have news for you: God is counting on you to birth His miracle! It is no wonder you have been feeling out of sorts, on the edge, and out of joint lately. You are changing. Your spiritual palate is changing too. You are no longer content to eat the spiritual food you used to eat. For some odd reason, you have a craving for something richer, something hotter, something you've never tasted before.

All of the evidence indicates that you are pregnant. In fact, you are ready to deliver something, and I'd better warn you that things will get messy in your life before they get better. The spiritual clothes you used to wear no longer fit you. It is time to break out of the politically correct restraints and give birth to the "God thing" in your heart.

Perhaps you didn't even know you were pregnant, but you know now. The seed of God's Word went straight into your spiritual womb, experienced a process of death, and then sprang forth to life by spontaneous generation of the Holy Spirit. The only way out of your predicament is to give birth to the miracle God planted in you.

Let me warn you that the process may not be pretty, and it definitely won't be "respectable" by religious standards. I went into the delivery room with my wife, Joni, when she was delivering our children. I honestly believe my wife is the most beautiful and tasteful woman on earth, but when she was in the delivery room for her thirty-sixth hour of labor, the perfume she put on two days earlier was only a faint memory. Her hairdresser wouldn't have recognized her.

SHE WANTED TO PUSH THAT BABY
FROM ONE WORLD INTO ANOTHER

The point is that it wasn't dress-up time; it was time for Joni to have her baby. She put her entire focus on one thing and one thing only—to push that baby from one world into another. I was just along for the ride, and it was all I could do to walk up and down the hallways for the first six hours. I didn't have the focus that Joni had because I wasn't carrying that baby. She had barely completed one-sixth of her labor when her big, strong husband said, "Baby, my legs are hurting. Are you bored? Do you want to go somewhere?" She didn't, but I had to go for Doritos twice.

Joni had very little patience with distractions from her central purpose in that place. At one point, my gentle, loving wife reached up and grabbed me by the collar and said, "Get your camel breath out of my face. *You* did this to me!"

Delivery isn't pretty and it isn't quiet, but every woman who endures it will tell you it was worth the price. As a male, the closest I will ever come to the pangs of childbirth is happening *right now*. I am in the grip of a conviction and a divine affliction. God put something in me that *has to come* out!

This third generation of ours is in dire need of revival. We sold out and compromised for convenience and the approval of man until we were no longer convinced that God's kingdom was worth the cost of pouring out our lives. All we had was an opinion, and we were falling apart. Then some of us got hungry. Desire drove us to intimacy with God, and we came out of His presence pregnant with His purposes! It was no accident.

Every new golden era of human history has been preceded by the devotion and righteous passion of one or more individuals who were willing to lay down their lives to birth God's purposes in their generation. It's time to head for the delivery room again.

CHROMIUM-PLATED CHRISTIANITY AND MATCHSTICK FIREPOWER

We're the third generation from Azusa Street. We're the third generation from pentecostal power, and our chromium-plated, overorganized, superstreamlined, and computerized form of Christianity has been just about as effective on our lost and hell-bound generation as the puny flame of a matchstick on an iceberg.

We boast about religious trivialities as if they represent a move of God while a large percentage of laity and leadership alike are bound by lust and unforgiveness. Meanwhile, rebellious rock stars baptized in blasphemy continue to poison a generation. Hollywood unleashes hundreds of films and a flood of immorality every year that have undermined our homes and blighted our youth.

The entertainment industry taps the best natural talent in America to create a television menu of everything foolish, vile, empty, and violent. Then the whole mess is packaged and promoted with incredible appeal and marketing savvy to deceive an entire generation.

In response, we take God's unspeakable glory and manifold cure to the world, but our false fruit bungles our presentation as though we were lying. The world has been lying well, and we've been telling the truth badly.

Therefore, we have drug-addicted mothers sitting on the fourth pew who put their next fix ahead of their children's next meal. We have fathers who put their drive for perverted sexual gratification ahead of their own daughters' need for common dignity. America has produced a warped generation that is convenience driven, not commitment driven. We make crucial decisions based on popular opinion rather than on solid biblical principles.

I refuse to continue to build on the faulty foundation of the self-help humanism that pabulum-pumping preachers perpetrate on this generation. No, we must return to the right foundation. Something is missing.

You know why the world doesn't want anything to do with what it perceives to be the church? Most of its man-centered religious routine is already dead; it just doesn't have enough good sense to lie down.

IT'S TIME FOR A REVOLUTION!

A preacher told me, "You know, Brother Rod, in the healing revival God did great miracles like that, but now He's doing another thing." I'm sorry, but I thought I was serving the One who changeth not. I don't think God is doing a new thing (by avoiding the performance of miracles). I think we are backslidden. It's time for a revolution.

Humanism, the reborn version of the old Greek heresy that "man is the measure of all things" (or "man is his own god"), has resurfaced in our day. Even the church has embraced many of its man-centered doctrines to form an unholy mixture that God refuses to tolerate in any form. He will not be satisfied to have people called by His name presume to add or take away from His holiness, His wisdom, His power, or His revealed Word. (He is, after all, a *holy God*.)

Nothing's missing? Where are Paul's handkerchiefs and aprons? Nothing's missing? How come the people in your church who don't tithe but steal God's money and then stand there and sing "Amazing Grace" don't fall dead on Sunday morning? Don't tell me nothing's missing. Of course, something's missing. I'll tell you what's missing. The divine life of God is missing.

The Bible says, "In him was life; and the life was the light of men" (John 1:4). I'm tired of seeing the church depend on the Dough Boys Quartet, Foofoo the Performing Dog, parking lot carnivals, slicky slides, and public swimming pools to bring in people. They may draw a crowd, but only the life-changing power of God can keep a crowd. I'm tired of user-friendly evangelism if it means we must make the gospel "palatable" to a hell-bound generation. Jesus said, "Strait is the gate, and narrow is the way, which leadeth unto life, and few there be that find it" (Matt. 7:14). I am positive He didn't add to His Word by authorizing a public works road-widening project for the road to heaven.

JESUS ESSENTIALLY PUT A RAZOR-WIRE FENCE AROUND THE KINGDOM

We should return to the kingdom entrance requirements decreed in God's Word: "If any man will come after me, let him deny himself, and take up his cross, and follow me. For whosoever will save his life shall lose it: and whosoever will lose his life for my sake shall find it" (Matt. 16:24–25). This is the spiritual equivalent of surrounding the church building with a twelve-foot chain-link fence topped with razor wire. The people who make it over Jesus' fence are the kind of volunteers you want in a foxhole with you. They won't sound retreat just because their headache isn't healed.

I come from eastern Kentucky, which is known as hillbilly country. God brought me out of the mountains of Kentucky to lead this ministry, and by His grace, I minister on national television, radio, and multiple forms of print media. I can still wear the same size hat every day because I remember where I came from, who brought me here, and who keeps me here. It is all by the grace of God.

The eastern region of Kentucky isn't known for its abundance of material wealth, but it is rich in old-fashioned common sense. As a boy, I learned that chickens cluck, dogs bark, cows moo, donkeys bray, and hogs grunt. These facts don't change, even though some rich folks like to dress up their pet hogs, baptize them in $100-an-ounce perfume, and plant them in La-Z-Boy recliners in their living rooms. They give these animals from the mud wallow their own remote controls to go with their own fifty-two-inch television screens. They think nothing of giving their pigs a cool Pepsi to drink while they paint their nails and pierce their ears.

PIGS LIKE MUD BECAUSE THEY ARE PIGS— WHAT YOU LOVE DEFINES WHO YOU ARE

Ask any eastern Kentucky boy what happens sooner or later. He'll tell you that as soon as that pig sees those folks turn their backs, he'll bolt out of their parlor and wallow in the first mud hole he can find. Why? Pigs like mud because they are pigs. You live what you are. Jesus put it this way: "Ye shall know them by their fruits" (Matt. 7:16).

If the grace of God transformed us, then we should live transformed lives. We don't have any business telling people that "the same spirit that raised up Christ from the dead now dwells inside my mortal body" if it is 9:00 A.M. and we're already getting tired of being in church.

Most of the people in the modern church have no shout and no dance, and they look as if they spent the night upside down in a posthole and were just baptized in vinegar. They have no vigor, no victory, no passion, and no conviction. They are living the *que sera, sera* life ("what will be, will be") while keeping company with a self-pity demon that constantly whines, "Why is everybody always picking on me?"

The church creates a deadly void when it ceases to be God's preserving salt and illuminating light in the world. Christian apathy and inaction trigger the escalation of every man-made (and devil-inspired) religious, political, and social movement conceivable, including communism, radical feminism, Marxism, and Nazism. This in turn breeds spiritual anarchy, physical and social mayhem, and ultimately martyrdom.

In contrast, a reawakening of the moral virtue of a people triggers a godly revolutionary movement. Revolutionary change becomes necessary only when the moral virtue and intelligence of the redeemed or the vice and ignorance of the damned demand it. As I noted earlier, at that point negotiation and compromise are void, and a revolution is inevitable.

WE CAN'T DEMAND RAIN WITHOUT THUNDER AND LIGHTNING

The entity perceived by the world to be the church isn't what it claims to be. It claims to uphold the cause of Christ, yet condemns confrontation. It is little more than a social club that demands rain without accepting the thunder and lightning. Its members practice the art of compromise and conciliation at all costs, avoiding confrontation by willingly dwelling in the devil's demilitarized zone to preserve their facade of peace.

Our entire culture is in chaos. The moral foundations originally constructed on the bedrock of the tenets of our faith are rapidly crumbling around us. We are stalled at a crossroad of crisis, stuck at a strategic inflection point that demands a choice.

As the third generation in the Spirit, we must choose to either experience revival (and pay the price of righteousness) or become but mere shells and shadows of our former selves. Men will tolerate anything until there is birthed within them a dynamic desire to change. Are you tired of going to church services where you shout, make a lot of noise, jump up and down, and then walk out unchanged? Something is missing, and it is the electrifying life of Christ. It is impossible to have an encounter with Him and leave unchanged! Let me tell you something:

If you're in some dead, cold place where exuberant worship of the King of kings is relegated to the Sunday night service, get out.

If you're going to a place where there's no shout, get out.

If you're going to a place where there's no victory, get out.

If you're going to a place where they never give an altar call, get out.

If you're going to a place where they never talk about the cleansing blood, the old rugged cross, and the glorious resurrection of Jesus Christ, get out, get out, get out!

The good news is that we aren't alone at this crossroads. A Shepherd is walking through the shadows of decision with us, and He has a glorious plan. If you recall, Jesus didn't leave the men on the road to Emmaus until He had revealed Himself to them. He left them only *after* the holy fire within Him ignited their hearts with unquenchable fire.

ARE YOU BURNING, OR ARE YOU JUST BURNED OUT?

Do you feel out of joint and out of position, as if something is missing from your life? Ask the Lord Jesus to give you a revelation of Himself, and stay in His presence until you forget there is anywhere else to be. Wait upon the Lord until His resurrection life hits your soul anew. It will ignite a fire of revival within you that will never go out.

When the fire of God ignites your desire, you will have eyes only for Him. You will act only through the power from above and speak only the things you received from your Father. The Master used this pattern to launch the first revolution almost two thousand years ago. Now He calls His remnant church to take up the same weapons of warfare.

Remnant believers with hearts afire can overcome even the greatest adversaries. They become the hands of God among men to restore the downhearted, lift up the downtrodden, and revive the life of Christ in the hearts of humanity.

God is looking for a remnant band with the faith to stand like Moses and point their fingers and declare through stuttering tongues with an anointing that staggers hell, "Let my people go!" When soldiers of an invading army hit a beachhead, they don't do it silently. They come in with a shout that strikes terror in the hearts of their adversaries. I dare you to declare to every demon trying to attack your life: "I'm coming out of status quo Christianity. Let the revolution begin!" Then pray, "Lord, blow on the embers of my soul and stir the fires of passion again. O God, do for me what I can't do for myself. In Jesus' name. Amen."

CHAPTER 6

AN INFALLIBLE
LEADER DIRECTS
THIS REVOLUTION

The most successful revolutionary leader in human history once asked his officers in training, "Whom do men say that I am?" Then he asked an even more important question: "But whom say ye that I am?"[1] Oddly enough, he asked those questions toward the end of his earthly campaign, after his men had spent nearly three years with him in the field. This revolutionary leader was Jesus Christ. He knew how important it was for His "officers," the disciples, to settle the matter in their hearts once and for all so they could never be persuaded otherwise in His absence. After that, Jesus began to share His plans for a cosmic revolution (Matt. 16:21).

The important factors haven't changed since then. Like the disciples, we live in a millennial era we can rightly call the fullness of time, and we are living on the brink of a holy revolution destined to transform our planet. The Lord is again training "officers" in His revolutionary remnant, and He asks each of us in turn, "Whom do men say that I am? Whom do *you* say that I am?"

Your answer to this question is crucial to your destiny. As noted earlier, God's revolutionary remnant people are irrevocably marked by four characteristics that can't be missed. They are (1) compelled by an inward desire, (2) to serve an infallible Leader, (3) through irresistible power, (4) based on absolute truth.

We looked closely at the purpose of inward desire in the hearts of God's people. It is the first step and prerequisite for the ignition of revolution through and in remnant people. The second component of holy revolution is no less important. This revolution is unique because its Leader is both divine and infallible. No ordinary human being will ever meet this qualification.

IDENTITY AND RECOGNITION BY REVELATION MEAN EVERYTHING

Think about the question the Lord asked the disciples, "But whom say ye that I am?" Wasn't the Lord ever announced or revealed to people before that moment? Identity and recognition by revelation mean everything where God's kingdom is concerned. We begin with Matthew's gospel:

> Now the birth of Jesus Christ was on this wise: When as his mother Mary was espoused to Joseph, before they came together, she was found with child of the Holy Ghost. Then Joseph her husband, being a just man, and not willing to make her a public example, was minded to put her away privily. But while he thought on these things, behold, the angel of the Lord appeared unto him in a dream, saying, Joseph, thou son of David, fear not to take unto thee Mary thy wife: for that which is conceived in her is of the Holy Ghost. And *she shall bring forth a son, and thou shalt call his name JESUS:* for he shall save his people from their sins. (Matt. 1:18–21, italics mine)

It is interesting to study the ways people name their children. I can still remember things said about my name one day when I was a boy riding in the car with my parents and my sister. Our parents told us the trip would take six hours, so my sister and I made a little bed on the backseat floor and settled in for the night. While I was waiting for the road vibrations to do their work and put me to sleep, my parents took advantage of the rare silence to talk between themselves.

WHAT IS HE GOING TO DO WHEN HE IS A MAN?

They began to talk about the time my sister was born, and they started talking about me (they had no idea I was still awake and all ears). I heard my dad say, "You know, I've been thinking about it, and I don't know what we've done." My mother said, "What do you mean?" Dad said, "Well, we named that boy Rodney. I was thinking about it at work the other day, and I thought, *Rodney. It's not too bad for a little boy, but what is he going to do when he is a man? They're going to be calling him Rodney.*"

My father's concern was real because we came from hillbilly country, and Rodney is not a hillbilly name. Buck and Beau are hillbilly names, but not Rodney. No one else in Kentucky was named Rodney but me (I was sure of it), and that disturbed me. That's the reason I asked people to call me Rod instead of Rodney.

Several years ago I visited Israel, and our guide handed me a little gift with Hebrew letters written on it. When I asked the woman what it said, she replied, "That is your name. They are the Hebrew letters corresponding to the English letters: R-O-H-I." I got excited because I knew that *Rohi* is one of the eight compound names of Jehovah. When you put *Jehovah* in front of *Rohi* in compound construction, you get *Jehovah-Rohi*, or "the Lord my God, my Shepherd." To say the least, I felt better about my name from that moment on.

Naming a child is exciting. Some names have biblical significance, but more times than not in modern times, they are a matter of preference. Names had much greater significance among the Old

Testament Hebrews, although things started off poorly. Adam and Eve named their firstborn son Cain, which means "acquired." Eve believed Cain was the promised seed, who would crush the serpent's head according to God's prophetic pronouncement in Eden. Obviously her hopes were disappointed. She named her second son Abel, which means "vanity," and she missed the mark there as well.

HOSEA PROPHESIED TO ISRAEL
THROUGH THE NAMES OF HIS CHILDREN

Hosea the weeping prophet married a prostitute at God's command, and gave his children names of great prophetic significance to his people: Jezreel (meaning "judgment is threatened"), Lo-ruhamah ("mercy is not obtained"), and Lo-ammi ("these are not my people").

In the passage I quoted from the first chapter of Matthew's gospel, an angel conveyed a name that God had registered as holy in heaven, and he decreed to Joseph God's perfect will concerning the boy who would bear that name. The name Jesus expressed the confidence God had in the child. God didn't relegate to Joseph or Mary the job of naming the Messiah. He sent an angel on a special assignment to say, "Thou shalt call his name JESUS: for he shall save his people from their sins" (Matt. 1:21).

Jesus was a very common name, and probably quite a few boys were living around Nazareth who also bore that name. When Joseph announced the name of Mary's infant son, it was similar to a modern American father announcing that his son's name will be John.

That name has a little more significance to us today, but it is clear that God specifically gave Jesus a common name to correspond with His incredible decision to leave His first estate of divinity to take on humanity and walk among us. He was so ordinary in outward appearance that those who grew up with Him refused to let Him break out of that box. They said, "Isn't this Jesus, the son of Joseph the carpenter?" (Matt. 13:55–57).

The revelation hidden in the common name of Jesus is simple: God the Son is not far off; He is right here where we are. He understands how we feel, and He knows what it is like to be tired, hungry, distressed, and in pain. He was one of us.

Without getting into all of the linguistic details, "Jesus" is an anglicized version of the Greek word *Iesous* (ee-ay-SOOCE). *Iesous* was based on a derivative of the ancient Hebrew name *Jehoshua* or *Joshua* ("Jehovah saved").[2] Despite its powerful meaning, Jesus' name was as common as James, John, or Bill today.

THE LIFE OF JOSHUA UNLOCKS THE REVELATION OF THE NAME OF JESUS

The first man in the Bible record to bear the name of Joshua appears in Exodus 17:9. The only way to grasp the power hidden in the common name of Jesus is to learn about Joshua. The name Joshua, or Jehoshua, doesn't seem to appear until Moses created it to replace Joshua's original name, Oshea ("deliverer"), in Numbers 13:16. Even this name change had prophetic significance.

When Joshua and the eleven other spies returned from Canaan, the majority report was, "Don't go in. We are not strong enough to defeat the enemies in the promised land." Only Caleb and Joshua believed God and urged the people to take the land (Num. 14:7–9). Even though Joshua's original name meant "deliverer" or "salvation," he was wise enough not to trust in his own strength and ability to deliver. He lived up to his new name, Jehoshua, which means "*Jehovah* saves." This young man was called Oshea when he came up out of Egypt. Nothing changed until Moses heard him declare his minority report.[3]

I can almost hear him declare to the Israelites: "Though I am

Oshea the deliverer, I am not the one who will deliver us. Yet I tell you that we are more than able to take the land because Jehovah is able to deliver us out of these circumstances. I am a mighty warrior, but I am unable to destroy the giants that are in the land. Put your trust in Jehovah, the great I AM whom I serve! He is the same Jehovah who brought us up out of the land of Egypt with His strong right arm. Jehovah sent us His servant Moses; and this Jehovah is well able to deliver us!"

THIS DELIVERER IS NO ORDINARY CHARACTER

In that moment Moses perceived that this man, Oshea, this deliverer, was no ordinary character. Then he received a revelation and said, "This man's name will no longer be called Oshea. I will call him *Jehoshua*." Under a prophetic unction, Moses coined the name Jehoshua by combining the divine name of God, *Jah*, with Oshea's given name, which means "deliverer" or "salvation." The result was a divinely inspired name that means "Jehovah delivers; Jehovah saves; Jehovah gets the victory." Jehoshua or Joshua became a common name as the centuries passed, but it was all part of God's plan.

The lives of Joshua and Jesus contain an amazing number of parallel situations of prophetic significance. Joshua embarked on his adult ministry from the wilderness, and Jesus did the same after overcoming Satan's temptations. Joshua became a great warrior and was chosen by God to lead the Israelites into the land of promise. Jesus was God's chosen Lamb and Warrior to lead His people into the kingdom of promise.

Another person named Joshua served as the high priest during the prophetic ministries of Haggai and Zechariah. The prophet Zechariah said the Lord showed him Joshua the high priest robed in filthy garments standing before an angel and Satan (Zech. 3:1–3). Joshua represents several things in the prophecy. First, he clearly represents the redeeming priest who symbolically carries the iniquities of his backslidden nation on his body as he goes before the Lord. His very name declares God's solution to Israel's sin: Jehovah will save.

I WILL BRING FORTH "THE BRANCH"

On another level, the angel of the Lord directed a command and a blessing directly to Joshua the high priest as a leader and priest to Israel. The angel also spoke of God's messianic promise to bring forth His servant, "the BRANCH" (Zech. 3:8).

Finally the Lord commanded Zechariah to make a crown of silver and gold and place it on Joshua's head before delivering this prophecy about the great Jehoshua, Yeshua, and Jesus:

> Behold the man whose name is The BRANCH; and he shall grow up out of his place, and he shall build the temple of the LORD: even he shall build the temple of the LORD; and he shall bear the glory, and shall sit and rule upon his throne; and he shall be a priest upon his throne: and the counsel of peace shall be between them both. (Zech. 6:12–13)

The mortal men known as Joshua, Jehoshua, and Jesus weren't fully successful in their lives or ministries. Joshua the son of Nun faithfully led the Israelites into the promised land and defeated all of their enemies, but he failed to lead Israel to a place of spiritual rest because the temporary atonement still depended on the works of the law and the inferior blood of animal sacrifices. Only in the finished work of Christ would God's people cease from their works and enter His rest.

Joshua the high priest played a key role as a repentant leader and a model of obedience in the ministries of Haggai and Zechariah. Yet in the end, the high priest failed in his mission because he couldn't fully remove the iniquity of the people.

HE CAME THROUGH A BORROWED WOMB

Centuries later, an angel of God announced the arrival of Jehovah's Salvation to Joseph. This Joshua, this Jehoshua, would save His people from their sin and cause them to enter His rest. In this *Christos,* in this "Anointed One," God's eternal name was eternally linked to what was common, for He came as a newborn baby, delivered through the birth canal and borrowed womb of a fourteen-year-old virgin woman.

We did not find Him; He came looking for us. Even when we answer God's call and seek His face, we must acknowledge that God gave us the "want to" and the "have to" of our spiritual hunger. God places eternal thirst in our hearts, even as He fills our every longing with His refreshing Spirit. We were full of the pulse of the world, and God made us hungry for the heavenly realm. We were drunk with the wine of humanity, yet God made us thirsty.

One name is the source of our deepest hunger and our strongest thirst. He is both our eternal longing and our blessed rest. Only this Deliverer can satisfy our hunger with His own flesh and slake our thirst with His own shed blood. Only this God-man can answer our longing for heaven by removing the hell in our hearts.

His name is common, but His name is also unspeakably holy. His name is Jesus, and it is as common as the name of John so we wouldn't be afraid to rub shoulders with Him (or drive nails into His hands and feet). Even so, divinity is wrapped up in the body of that carpenter from Nazareth. John the Beloved painted a portrait of God's grace in three acts: Act I, The Beginning (the gospel of John); Act II, The Life of the Family (John's epistles: 1, 2, and 3 John); and

Act III, The End (John's Revelation of Jesus Christ). The first act, the gospel of John, mirrors the beauty of the first words of Genesis, the Book of Beginnings:

> In the beginning was the Word, and the Word was *with God,* and the Word *was God.* The same was in the beginning with God . . . And *the Word was made flesh, and dwelt among us,* (and we beheld his glory, the glory as of the only begotten of the Father,) full of grace and truth. (John 1:1–2, 14, italics mine)

UNTIL JESUS CAME, WE COULD VIEW OUR CREATOR ONLY FROM A DISTANCE

Do you see the wonder of it all? After Adam sinned and was banished from God's intimate presence in the Garden, we could view our Creator only from the outside looking into Paradise. Sin separated and distanced us from His love. Our only approach to our deepest longing was through the law, and through the blood of sheep and goats offered to an invisible God who dwelt in darkness concealed from our view.

Then Jesus came in the flesh and dwelt among men as a common man. In Him, God and man sat down together in the inner court. One thing remained: Jesus had to sacrifice His life to pay the price for our sin and remove the dividing veil. John's gospel describes the third wonder that was prophesied of old: "Jesus answered and said unto him, If a man love me, he will keep my words: and my Father will love him, and *we will come unto him, and make our abode with him*" (John 14:23, italics mine).

Another man with the common name of David wrote this prophecy under the anointing and described the infallible Leader of God's revolutionary remnant army:

This is the generation of them that seek him, that seek thy face, O Jacob. Selah. Lift up your heads, O ye gates; and be ye lifted up, ye everlasting doors; and the King of glory shall come in. *Who is this King of glory?* The LORD strong and mighty, the LORD mighty in battle. Lift up your heads, O ye gates; even lift them up, ye everlasting doors; and the King of glory shall come in. *Who is this King of glory?* The LORD of hosts, he is the King of glory. (Ps. 24:6–10, italics mine)

Who is this infallible Leader? Who is this King of kings and Lord of lords? Who has the wisdom, knowledge, power, and strength to lead such a revolution? It is the King of glory who "filleth all in all" (Eph. 1:23).

WE DIDN'T DARE APPROACH HIM, SO HE CAME TO US AS A BABY

When we beheld Him through Isaiah's eyes, we couldn't see Him or communicate with Him because He was so high and lifted up. The train of His unrestrained glory filled the temple, so we didn't dare approach Him (Isa. 6:1). Yet we *had to* get close to Him. Then suddenly He came to us as a baby in the tiny, forgotten village of Bethlehem, the ancient home of a psalmist shepherd named David. It was here we first discovered God wrapped up in swaddling clothes. It was here that man first beheld His glory embodied in living flesh.

John saw Jesus, "the fullness of the Godhead bodily" (Col. 2:9), with his own eyes and touched Him with his own hands. Then the apostle removed the "veil" through his gospel account so that we could see Him in a new light as the Son of man. He saw how the Son walked and talked, and he observed His mode of operation. That was how he realized that Jesus wasn't like other men. He could walk on water and make men speak who had not had the ability to speak. John learned that it was His will to heal, and he saw Him cast out demons with a word. The disciples saw Jesus rebuke the wind, and "they feared exceedingly, and said one to another, *What manner of man is this,* that even the wind and the sea obey him?" (Mark 4:41, italics mine).

THERE IS DIVINE IRONY IN THE
ANGEL'S WORDS TO JOSEPH

Jesus shared His common name with many other males in Israel. The divine irony appears in the angel's words to Joseph: "And thou shalt call his name JESUS: for he shall save his people from their sins" (Matt. 1:21). Again, please understand that except for the *historic significance* of the name, the angel's words, "You shall call his name Jesus . . . ," meant no more than if he had said, "You shall call his name John."

Outward appearance can conceal the inward reality, and God counted on the fact that we are *not* like Him. He once warned Samuel the prophet, "Look not on his countenance, or on the height of his stature; because I have refused him: for the LORD seeth not as man seeth; for man looketh on the outward appearance, but the LORD looketh on the heart" (1 Sam. 16:7).

God wrapped divinity in a blanket of fragile humanity and gave His only begotten Son a common and easily forgotten name. He ordained before the foundations of the world that His Son would invade our world from the birthplace of kings—tiny Bethlehem— where David was anointed king by the prophet (1 Sam. 16). In this way, only people with eyes to see and ears to hear would perceive the infant Messiah's true identity.

Where Joshua the great captain and leader failed, Jesus would succeed. Although Joshua the great high priest wore tattered garments of iniquity and symbolically bore the sins of the people, he failed to remove their sins or convince them to remain faithful to their God. Jesus the Great High Priest would succeed by coming to "indwell" or "tabernacle" with His people.

This Joshua from heaven is unlike any other, for He saved His people from their sin. When John the Baptist saw the uncommon man with the common name come to the river Jordan, he told his disciples, "Behold the Lamb of God, which taketh away the sins of the world" (John 1:29). John, the greatest of the prophets, had been preparing for that moment all of his life. It was his duty to pull away the veil from the common to reveal the Divine—whether anyone listened or not.

THIS JOSHUA SUCCEEDED WHERE ALL OTHERS HAD FAILED

This time, Joshua, "Jehovah saves," would succeed where all others had failed. He will take us triumphantly through our conflicts, and He will bring us to His rest. He did more than merely remove the garments of our iniquity; He removed them as far as the east is from the west *to be remembered against us no more* (Ps. 103:12).

Although the baby grew up without sin, He still carried that common name through adolescence and the length of His adult ministry on the earth. He carried the forgettable name of a common man even as He dragged an old rugged cross through the jeering crowds and winding streets of Jerusalem to Golgotha, the place of execution.

All of heaven's hosts must have watched in awe as Jehoshua, Jehovah's Salvation, offered up His flesh to the worst tortures known to the skilled Roman executioners. Could He do it? Could He truly refuse to call upon His power and right of divinity despite the unjust punishment and pain? Could He break the ancient penalty of sin and bring God's creation into eternal rest? Would He pave the way with His own flesh and blood so fallen men and women could fulfill their divine purpose in the earth? The angelic hosts gasped as they watched Him wheezing while the killing weight of His mangled earthly body pressed down against His lungs. Then finally He drew a ragged breath and cried to the darkening heavens, "It is finished" (John 19:30).

This Joshua, this divine emissary, did not look back or turn back from His Father's mission of redemption. Jesus, Jehoshua, exploded from a borrowed tomb on the third day, having spoiled the enemy in the lower parts of the earth and led captivity captive. He destroyed the power of death, hell, and the grave; and He carried that common name up out of the fire-baked walls of the devil's perdition (Eph. 4:9–10).

JESUS RETURNED TO HEAVEN TO RECEIVE AN HONOR HELD BY NO OTHER

Jesus waded through hell's hordes and ripped the keys of demonic authority from Satan's paralyzed hands before returning to our realm in an unequaled release of divine energy and light. Then He ministered to the disciples for forty days, preparing the first messianic remnant army for their world-changing task (Acts 1:3). Finally Jesus, *Jehoshua,* returned to the presence of His Father in heaven to receive an honor possessed by no other:

> Wherefore God also hath highly exalted him, and given him a name which is above every name: *that at the name of Jesus every knee should bow,* of things in heaven, and things in earth, and things under the earth; *and that every tongue should confess that Jesus Christ is Lord,* to the glory of God the Father. (Phil. 2:9–11, italics mine)

When *this* Joshua completed His heavenly mission, something happened to that common name. The Resurrected Man resurrected the divine origin and meaning and power of His common name. Then He gave His name and the power vested in that name to the common people who gave Him their lives:

Hitherto have ye asked nothing in my name: *ask, and ye shall receive, that your joy may be full.* These things have I spoken unto you in proverbs: but the time cometh, when I shall no more speak unto you in proverbs, but I shall show you plainly of the Father. *At that day* ye shall ask *in my name* . . . (John 16:24–26, italics mine)

Power is in the name of Jesus. Victory, deliverance, and healing are in His name. Joy unspeakable and full of glory is in His name. Help and a future are in His name. Best of all, this is the name of our infallible Leader: Jesus, Jehovah our Salvation. This is the Leader whom John described in the Revelation, the book at the *end of the Book:*

I saw heaven opened, and behold a white horse; and *he that sat upon him was called Faithful and True,* and in righteousness he doth judge and make war. His eyes were as a flame of fire, and on his head were many crowns; *and he had a name written, that no man knew, but he himself.* And he was clothed with a vesture dipped in blood: and *his name is called The Word of God.* And the armies which were in heaven followed him upon white horses, clothed in fine linen, white and clean. And out of his mouth goeth a sharp sword, that with it he should smite the nations: and he shall rule them with a rod of iron: and he treadeth the winepress of the fierceness and wrath of Almighty God. And *he hath on his vesture and on his thigh a name written, KING OF KINGS, AND LORD OF LORDS.* (Rev. 19:11–16, italics mine)

We have longed for this infallible Leader, the King of glory destined to lead His revolutionary remnant army to the very gates of hell to snatch millions of souls out of Satan's deathly grip! Behold our unfailing Savior and Leader: "He hath done all things well" (Mark 7:37).

CHAPTER 7

IRRESISTIBLE POWER
PRODUCES IRREPRESSIBLE
REVOLUTION

In 1976, I was a fairly successful Baptist pastor with a congregation of about 150 people in Columbus, Ohio. I already had a strong inward desire to serve my infallible Leader, Jesus Christ. But I didn't know that God wanted to introduce me to the crucial third component of His plan for revolutionary remnant people.

We were already known for our love for God and one for another, and we believed God's Word. We knew how to work hard and faithfully in the kingdom, and we knew how to serve one another. The only problem was that *there was no power* in our lives beyond the power released when individuals surrendered their lives to Christ. That is a wonderful thing, and I would never belittle that life-transforming miracle. However, God wanted to show me there was *more.*

That was the year my sister was sent home to die after suffering severe injuries in an automobile crash. She was taking thirty-five prescribed medications per day, but her doctor told us privately, "We'll just give her several bottles of Demerol and some needles.[1] She should give herself a shot when she can't stand the pain any longer. The best thing you can do is try to keep her as comfortable as you can."

During the time my sister hovered on the brink of death, I learned that my mother had an incurable heart condition. Right in the middle of that crisis, a family friend told me, "Your sister can live and not die."

"I don't really know about that," I said. He nodded and said, "She can live and not die—*if* you will take her to a special meeting in Indianapolis, Indiana." Our family was desperate by that time. We realized the doctors felt the end was near when they changed their focus from treatment to mere pain management. Medical science had exercised the last of its options; my sister needed nothing less than a miracle.

We had nothing to lose and everything to gain, so we decided to take my sister to that meeting. To make a long story short, we stayed there all week and spent every day in church. We sat on hard folding chairs hour after hour for only one reason: something *powerful* was going on there.

GOD PLACED HIS HEALING POWER IN MY HANDS

In that meeting God placed His healing power in my hands. There God first taught me the New Testament doctrine of laying hands on the sick. That week, this Baptist preacher *prophesied* for the first time, even though I didn't know what it was! I was so embarrassed by what happened that I went to the guest minister after the meeting and said, "I'm really sorry for what happened; I don't know what came over me. I don't know why I said all that stuff and then said, 'Thus saith the Lord' at the end."

That brother looked at me with a twinkle in his eye and said, "Don't you know what that is?" I nodded and said, "Yes, it's called *being out of order.*" He grinned and said, "No, that is the gift of prophecy!"

If that wasn't enough to shake up my life, something happened on the final night of the meeting that changed my life forever. The guest minister, Norvel Hayes, wrapped his arms around my desperately sick sister and held her for two hours and forty-five minutes while he prayed for God to deliver her. At the end of that time, God's glory shot over the sapphire sill of heaven and flooded the earth and instantly set my sister free! I had never seen the power of God invade the world of man like that, but I knew beyond a shadow of a doubt that it was the real thing.

GET UP! GOD IS GOING TO HEAL YOU!

I was a changed man when I stepped behind the pulpit of our Baptist church the following Sunday morning. I looked across the congregation and sensed a new measure of faith that morning. Then I said, "From now on, anything that happened in Matthew, Mark, Luke, or John is not only possible, but it is probable in this church! If you are sick, I want you to know that God has placed His healing power in my hands. Now get up and come down here. God is going to heal you."

Until I made that announcement, only one person had ever been slain in the Spirit or fallen under the power of God in our services. We knew that kind of thing could happen, and if it did, we probably wouldn't approve of it. All I did was to reach out to pat a woman on the head one time and she fell over! We promptly called for an ambulance, and I thought, *Oh, dear God, I'm just getting started in this thing, and I've already killed a woman.*

The power of God invaded our little Baptist church that day, and things were about to change. Every sick person in that building jumped to his feet. People filled the center aisle and the front altar area. No one was ready for what happened next. Evidently God wanted the people to know that the demonstrations of divine power they would see in the days ahead were from Him and no one else. I can tell you this: all of the people who made it to the front row stopped acting like good Baptists. The power of God hit them, and they reacted exactly as if they had run into a wall.

This kind of thing just didn't happen in our church, and the people in my congregation didn't go someplace to learn how to act this way. The rest of the people in the congregation got up and started running to the front. Once again, as soon as they reached the front row, the power of God hit them so hard that they looked as if they had been hit in the head with a sledgehammer! Those people fell on top of each other until bodies were stacked as high as the top of the seat on the front row.

BAPTISTS AREN'T KNOWN FOR
ROLLING AROUND HELPLESSLY

Perhaps you don't know this, but Baptists are not known for falling on top of each other like kindling wood and rolling around helplessly. We avoid that kind of thing like the plague, but God ambushed the entire church that day. As soon as those who were sick stood up, God healed them. Then He decided to baptize that whole room full of Baptists in the mighty baptism in the Holy Spirit with the evidence of speaking in other tongues. (He didn't sprinkle us either; He dunked us. And *we didn't pray for that to happen!*)

The Holy Spirit is invisible, unstoppable, and unpredictable. He is like the wind: we don't see Him coming, and we don't see Him leave. Most of the time, we perceive only the effect of His arrival and the void created by His departure.

From the Scriptures, we can recognize another manifestation of His presence. When He comes in power to empower His people or answer their unified prayers, He can shake houses, jails, mountains, or the earth itself. When He comes in judgment or correction, the

Bible says the Holy Spirit will shake everything that can be shaken (Heb. 12:27).

God wants you to be "possessed" by the Holy Spirit. When the Holy Spirit totally dominates your life, you will give no place to the world, to the flesh, or to the devil. He sanctifies or sets you apart in spirit, soul, and body.

GOD'S BREATH RAISES THE DEAD THINGS BACK TO LIFE

The anointing is Holy Spirit possession. He is the very anointing of God working through you in deliverance and inner strength you never knew existed. God is about to breathe on us again, and every "dead thing" His breath touches comes to life once again. His holy inspiration will revive your seemingly dead hunger for His Holy Word, prayer, worship, and His presence: "As the hart panteth after the water brooks, so panteth my soul after thee, O God. My soul thirsteth for God, for the living God: when shall I come and appear before God?" (Ps. 42:1–2).

You will love people you couldn't love before God's Holy Spirit possessed you. You will say things you couldn't say before, and you will live and minister on levels you never knew before.

A Holy Spirit anointing will come upon the church as it passes through the "birth canal" of God-ordained change and emerges as a brand-new "being" never before seen on this planet. This revolutionary remnant church is so possessed by the Holy Spirit that it sees with the piercing vision of the Spirit, walks with Holy Spirit steps, speaks with the tongue and authority of God's Spirit, and operates according to the *knowledge* of the Holy Spirit. Yes, we have experienced the power and wonder of a little charismatic renewal, but we are about to experience total Holy Spirit possession!

"Can two walk together, except they be agreed?" (Amos 3:3).

Two can walk together only when both parties make a conscious decision to walk together and allow nothing to come between them. We need to agree with the Holy Spirit and walk with Him.

"That is impossible in this day and time! We are bombarded with temptations and opposition from every side." No, we are an "Enoch generation." We know from God's Word that in the midst of an evil and perverse age, Enoch "had this testimony, that he pleased God" (Heb. 11:5).

WE POSSESS HIS POWER
ONLY AFTER HE POSSESSES US!

The irresistible power of the Holy Spirit is available to each of us, but only on God's terms. We can possess the power of God only after we allow Him to totally possess us. Have you ever wondered what life would be like if you were in absolute agreement with God by His Spirit? You could clean out your medicine cabinets, cancel your counseling appointments, and permanently postpone your doctors' visits. You and I aren't there yet, so we need to be praying for the physicians, pharmacists, and other health professionals God sends into our lives. They are a valuable part of God's provision for a church on the grow.

I deeply appreciate doctors and other health professionals; they do the best they can with the natural and technological resources available to them. However, I look forward by faith to the day when their primary service to God's kingdom will be to confirm the supernatural intervention of God in divine healing, restoration or creation of body parts, and countless resurrections from the dead!

The days of option are gone. The days of our amalgamation of the world, the flesh, and the things of darkness with our holy God are over. We have reached one of the most momentous and world-changing strategic inflection points in recorded human history. We are confronted by a divine dividing line and commanded to make a choice.

The Israelites had to decide between crossing the river Jordan into the unseen destiny of God's promises or remaining in the wilderness without the promises. We face the same choice in the Spirit.

We may not like it, but we must go with God all the way or forget following Him altogether. Part-timers need not apply. Halfhearted participants may be left behind because the pace of God's purposes is too great for the uncommitted and unchanged. This relentless process is just part of God's plan to give birth to a revolutionary people destined to possess the land with *irresistible power*.

GOD PLANS TO MAKE US A WONDER!

"Joshua said unto the people, Sanctify yourselves: for tomorrow *the LORD will do wonders among you*" (Josh. 3:5, italics mine). God issued the same call to His revolutionary remnant church. He plans to "make us a wonder" to the world for His own glory. This is a divine pattern of conquest and restoration.

The prophet Isaiah declared, "Behold, *I and the children whom the LORD hath given me are for signs and for wonders* in Israel from the LORD of hosts, which dwelleth in mount Zion" (Isa. 8:18, italics mine). Jesus is saying the same thing about us today. He intends to so completely sanctify or separate us from the world, the flesh, and the devil that people around us will look at us in wonder.

The harvest of souls did not end with the passing of the previous millennium. It has only begun. God is giving birth to a revolutionary remnant people who are *possessed* by an irresistible power. I am convinced that we are going to reenact the book of Acts in the days to come, but God cannot do it through everyone. It might as well be us and it might as well be here and it might as well be now.

If we yield to Him, God will lead us into the realm of the spirit and release His power in our everyday lives to do the following:

1. Overcome sin and bad habits.

2. Cast out demons and exercise power over all the authority of the devil.

3. Call for angelic protection.

4. Heal the sick.

5. Destroy the works of Satan.

6   Work miracles.

7. Expose and execute judgment upon false prophets.

8. Receive revelation knowledge.

9. Do the works of Jesus and greater works through the Holy Spirit.

10. Walk in the fruit of the Spirit.

THE ORDINARY CHRISTIAN IS POSSESSED!

In the eyes of God, the only ordinary Christian is an extraordinary, supernatural Christian possessed by the Spirit. In fact, the Bible uses the interesting term "seven Spirits" in four separate passages of the book of Revelation (1:4; 3:1; 4:5; 5:6). The first passage reads,

> John to the seven assemblies (churches) that are in Asia: May grace (God's unmerited favor) be granted to you and spiritual peace (the peace of Christ's kingdom) from Him Who is and Who was and Who is to come, and from the seven Spirits [*the sevenfold Holy Spirit*] before His throne [Isa. 11:2]. (Rev. 1:4 AMPLIFIED, italics mine).

Isaiah made it clear why the "seven Spirits" (or sevenfold Holy Spirit of God) are so important to us today. He pierced the veil of time to describe the coming Messiah when he said, "And *the spirit of the LORD* shall rest upon him, the *spirit of wisdom* and *understanding,* the *spirit of counsel* and *might,* the *spirit of knowledge* and of *the fear of the LORD*" (Isa. 11:2, italics mine).

Each of these seven manifestations of the Holy Spirit should be operating in our lives. The first, *the spirit of the Lord,* is operating in every born-again, blood-washed saint saved from sin and death through the death and resurrection of Jesus Christ. The Holy Spirit always points our hearts, our minds, and our desires toward Jesus, the Son of God. It is no accident that this spirit or manifestation of the Spirit is listed first.

ILLUMINATED WITH GOD'S UNDERSTANDING

The second, *the spirit of wisdom,* is different from the gift of "the *word* of wisdom" described in 1 Corinthians 12:8. The first term refers to an aspect of the Holy Spirit continuously at work in us day and night. The second refers to a gift that is activated by the Spirit only to meet a need in the body or to be a sign and wonder to a non-Christian. We may operate in the gift of the word of wisdom as the Spirit wills, but we are totally possessed by God's spirit of wisdom.

The spirit of understanding also operates continuously, and it refers to the ability to perceive and grasp the nature of a thing or situation and how it relates to the kingdom of light and the kingdom of darkness.

People possessed by *the spirit of counsel* demonstrate a continuous flow of God's supernatural wisdom in their lives. They seem to have a God-given ability to pierce the fog and confusion surrounding the affairs of men and provide wise counsel in the midst of confusion.

The spirit of might seemed to possess Dr. Lester Sumrall right up until the day he suddenly went to be with the Lord. He could wear out forty-two twenty-year-olds when he was eighty years old! The fire of God seemed to burn so brightly in him that he was fueled by God's passion and glory. I don't know why so many people in this modern age complain about being tired. "How are you doing today?" "Well, I'm tired." What did they do to be so fatigued—breathe too hard?

We need to be possessed by the spirit of might. Every week people ask me, "How do you live and do all the things you do?" I preach approximately 250 times a year; I oversee the operations and ministry of World Harvest Church, Breakthrough Media Ministries, and a growing Bible college; and I tape seemingly endless television programs. I also have my duties as a husband and as a father to two children (one of whom is a child with special needs).

I have a hard time sympathizing with healthy people who complain about trying to walk in the Spirit after working from eight o'clock to five o'clock. The problem is that most Christians constantly live in the natural realm. You can plant yourself in front of your television set and watch CNN, but don't expect victory to come that way. Do you want Holy Spirit power in your life? Pull away from the distractions of the day, and pray in the Holy Spirit. Lock yourself in your prayer closet, and pray until the power comes down.

People who are possessed by *the spirit of knowledge,* as Jesus was, seem to continually know things they have no obvious way of knowing. It is as if God constantly speaks secrets to them through an unseen earpiece.

Jesus perfectly demonstrated *the spirit of the fear of the Lord.* Even though He was God the Son, He demonstrated a fear or reverent awe of His heavenly Father in everything He did. His earthly life and ministry were built around His continual acknowledgment of His Father's authority, purpose, will, and holiness. People possessed by this spirit refuse to defile the things of the house of God or speak lightly of dignitaries or the people of God.

God wants all of us to be possessed by the Holy Spirit—with all seven of His attributes mentioned in Revelation 1:4 and Isaiah 11:2. Too many of us claim to be baptized in the Holy Spirit, though we are more dead than alive, more off than on, and more wrong than right! We have become Spirit-*frilled,* but not Spirit-*filled.* We are strangers to the inner essence of His power because we have grown accustomed to living on the outer fringe of God's works.

We ignore the Holy Spirit more than we deny Him. Peter prayed for ten days before he preached his ten-minute message on the day of pentecost and saw thousands swept into God's kingdom. Today, we preach for ten days after praying for only ten minutes. No wonder we have so many failures!

WE PREFER MIRACLES OVER MARKETING

Times are changing. God is raising a great revolutionary remnant in the church. This army of the hungry is ready to trade its dignity for demonstration and will gladly swap its academic degrees for divine revelation. The people in this army prefer miracles over marketing and value repentance more than reputation. Frankly all we need is another drenching downpour of pentecostal power from on high.

I'm not talking about the supernatural work of the Holy Spirit that transforms our lives when we repent and receive Jesus Christ as Lord and Savior. That is the minimum prerequisite for the mighty baptism in the Holy Spirit.

If you have a pentecostal, charismatic, or full-gospel background, this may be old news to you. However, for Baptist people like me, or for Presbyterians, Episcopalians, Methodists, Congregationalists, Roman Catholics, and countless others, this is something new and glorious from heaven's door.

We didn't think this thing existed anymore, but then something issued over the sapphire sill of heaven's gate and went through us from the top of our heads to the bottoms of our feet. It did for us what a phone booth did for Clark Kent. The Holy Spirit changed us into another class of human beings, endued from on high with power to be witnesses for the King. I know this much: it is a lifelong condition we will never set aside.

IT CAME TO PASS IN THE FULLNESS OF TIME

The prophets knew it was coming. Isaiah spoke of "stammering lips" and "another tongue" (Isa. 28:11). Zechariah prophesied metaphorically that the Spirit would fall like rain (Zech. 10:1). Amos knew it would take some preparation (Amos 4:12); Hosea said it would take the breaking up of fallow ground (Hos. 10:12); and Malachi knew that He would come suddenly to His temple (Mal. 3:1). Sure enough, it came to pass in the fullness of time:

> Suddenly there came a sound from heaven as of a rushing mighty wind, and it filled all the house where they were sitting. And there appeared unto them cloven tongues like as of fire, and it sat upon each of them. And they were all filled with the Holy Ghost, and began to speak with other tongues, as the Spirit gave them utterance. (Acts 2:2–4)

We need something to happen suddenly in the church this very day! Powerless pentecost has become the norm and not the exception. We need the power, but few of us want to count the cost of receiving the real thing. I remember a day before the charismatic renewal when it was not popular to be a pentecostal. Now we find ourselves entangled in the First Church of the Politically Correct and the Professionally Expedient, where we prefer not to talk about the tongues thing or the gifts of the Spirit.

We still need to count the cost of the power of pentecost! The only way to fulfill our divine mandate as God's revolutionary remnant people is to walk and minister in Holy Spirit power. The Upper Room experience known as the baptism in the Holy Spirit produced power in the disciples' lives, but it also propelled them into prison cells. They were endued with power from on high, but they were also banished from the organized religion of the day.

John the Baptist said, "I indeed baptize you with water unto repentance: but he that cometh after me is mightier than I, whose shoes I am not worthy to bear: he shall baptize you with the Holy Ghost, and with fire" (Matt. 3:11).

This is my final warning in this controversial chapter: once the fire of the Holy Spirit touches your tongue with the burning coal of God, you will no longer be content to dance to the rigors of religiosity. The fire shut up in your bones will explode in your life and force its way out through your words, actions, and daring deeds of faith in Christ as a ragged revolutionary remnant believer.

You will no longer fit in with the crowd because the flames of renewed passion will mark you as one *possessed* by the blessed Holy Spirit of God! Why? Because God imparts His irresistible power to us to produce an irrepressible revolution on a cosmic scale.

CHAPTER 8

ABSOLUTE TRUTH
IS THE FOUNDATION
FOR REVOLUTION

For centuries, the church has thrived on three of the four characteristics of a revolutionary remnant people. Its members were
compelled by an inward desire to *serve an infallible Leader* based on
absolute truth. They lacked the *irresistible power* available through
the baptism of the Holy Spirit and never could trigger a global revolution to match God's plan.

Most of our churches held to the basic bedrock of biblical doctrine as well (although most chose to ignore the "pentecostal" passages on the baptism of the Holy Spirit and the gifts in the book of
Acts, Ephesians 4, 1 Corinthians 12, and Romans 12), until the evo-
lution controversy rocked America and shook the foundations of
many unstable believers.

Some of us permitted the power of the Holy Spirit to reenter
our personal lives and our churches, but the age of relative humanism blossomed in the world, and many in the American church lost
their grip on the absolute truth of God's Word. Seeking to become
wise in the world's eyes, we became fools by drifting from our moor-
ing in absolute truth. We replaced our diet of spiritual discipline and

the pure meat of the Word with a smorgasbord spread of greasy grace, sweet platitudes, and boneless spiritual chicken. Solid Bible-based doctrine disappeared from our "pulpit menus" as did the fruits of stability in the faith.

The time is overdue for us to return to the discarded values of the past. God is about to instigate a riot and launch a resounding revolution designed to get us back to where we started. We must return to our first love by loving God first and putting His Word above every human notion and man-centered ideology, doctrine, and creed. As with most things in God's kingdom, our deviation from absolute truth begins in the beginning. In this case, it began in the nursery with our children.

ARE YOU A SUNDAY SCHOOL VETERAN?

Did you ever attend something called Sunday school? If you did, you may well be in your late thirties or older. Let me refresh your memory: most Sunday school veterans remember the unique smells of a Sunday school room in the old church basement and the bird-egg blue paint on the cinder-block walls. Do you have any memories of Sunday school? You may think I am being facetious, but you would be surprised at how few churches go to the trouble to maintain Sunday school classes in this selfish, self-centered age.

Do you remember the name of your Sunday school teacher? To preserve her privacy, I will call my instructor in the faith, my untiring tutor in the doctrines of eternity, Sister Gillicuddy. At that time, dear Sister Gillicuddy had not learned that the clothing industry made undergarments specifically designed to support the upper hemisphere of the female anatomy (but we were too young to care or understand).

We barely noticed her unique way of rolling up her knee hose or the way the fleshy part of her underarm moved when she used the familiar blue flannelgraph in Sunday school class. We secretly wondered why Sister Gillicuddy piled up her hair in such a tight bun, but she kept us so busy learning God's Word that we didn't have time to speculate on such a minor question.

No matter how hard you look in most churches today, you can't find a Sister Gillicuddy anywhere. She is probably lying in a tanning bed or getting her hair done—unless she is having her artificial nails done for forty-five dollars each.

YOU CAN'T FIND SISTER GILLICUDDY ANYMORE

As a consequence, our children don't know anything because we replaced Sunday school with the one-size-does-all junior church. We have incorporated every amusement and entertainment known to man in our children's programs, but our children still think the Epistles are the wives of the apostles. They don't know the Ten Commandments because there was no one available to teach them (but they can recite their favorite fast-food menus and the Saturday television cartoon lineup from memory).

They don't know it's not right to steal because no one sacrificed enough to teach them. Our teenagers sleep around in the backseats of '95 Chevys and '92 Fords because no one taught them it was wrong. I thank God for Sister Gillicuddy's determined instruction in the things of God. She taught me the politically incorrect facts about the Lord's return and the "catching away" of the saints. I didn't get in the backseat of a '74 Chevy on prom night because I was afraid Jesus might split the eastern sky before I climbed back in the front seat!

Sister Gillicuddy taught me the right way to live so I knew I had to live right. She was a crucial partner with my parents who also taught me these things. Together with the Holy Spirit, they made up a powerful team that had a way of driving home those points with a supernatural ability.

We don't have very many unwavering saints today because we

don't have many Sister Gillicuddys, and Sunday school instruction is a thing of the past. People frequently ask me how I can quote so many scripture passages from memory when I preach. Well, I didn't start yesterday. I started in *Sunday school.* "Brother Parsley, what seminary did you attend?" I graduated with honors from Sister Gillicuddy's Sunday School of the Bible and Sound Doctrine.

SHE KNEW THREE SCRAWNY KIDS
WERE WAITING FOR HER

Sister Gillicuddy was the saint who taught us discipline and the way to act in the house of God. She taught us to respect authority, respect God, respect God's Word, respect God's chosen leaders, and respect God's church. You would never catch Sister Gillicuddy wearing her dress fourteen inches above her knee, and you couldn't call her with the hottest gossip on Saturday night. She knew three scrawny kids were going to be waiting for her the following morning in that room with the blue walls, and it was her responsibility to teach them the gospel.

I was one of those little kids. More knees and elbows than anything else, I was from "that hillbilly bunch of Parsleys down yonder," and Sister Gillicuddy felt it was her responsibility to teach me about Shadrach, Meshach, and Abednego. She made me memorize countless scripture passages such as:

> Let not your heart be troubled: ye believe in God, believe also in me. In my Father's house are many mansions: if it were not so, I would have told you. I go to prepare a place for you. And if I go and prepare a place for you, I will come again, and receive you unto myself; that where I am, there ye may be also. (John 14:1–3)

Sister Gillicuddy did her job somehow without the benefit of balloons, videotapes, field trips, fun fairs, or weekly sweet treats.[1] Our only special activity came at Easter when my daddy set up a homemade Ping-Pong table made with a four-by-eight-foot sheet of plywood and some saw benches. My mother and the church women used to gather around that Ping-Pong table to stuff bags with treats for Easter.

SISTER GILLICUDDY HAD A DIVINE ASSIGNMENT

That was the only day Sister Gillicuddy would let anything interrupt her class because *she had a divine assignment*. She was going to make a preacher who would preach to 97 percent of America's households, 78 percent of Canada's households, and three hundred nations of the world. Her ministry then was as vital as my ministry is today, and it has always been that way in God's eyes.

I am also a product of one of the greatest youth groups in the world. Do you know what we learned in our youth group? We learned how to praise God, how to pray, and how to witness. We didn't have video games; we got our fun by going out to *impose the kingdom*.[2]

At World Harvest Church, we tried to minister to our children and teens using entertainment and fun activities, but we noticed that the good kids started acting like the bad kids. Even though we had nearly two thousand kids attending those meetings, I told them to shut the thing down. I would rather have two hundred who know how to reach God than have two thousand come in there merely to look for someone of the opposite sex.

We don't have very many Sister Gillicuddys anymore because we can't find enough people who are willing to sit in the church basement and talk to our world changers of the next generation. They are all too busy with their notepads and tape series. It is my responsibility as the pastor of our local church body to change that mind-set through the preaching of sound doctrine and instruction from God's Word.

A FOUNDATION OF SOUND DOCTRINE MUST BE LAID

I am responsible before God to lay a foundation by preaching "the principles of the doctrine of Christ . . . the foundation of repentance from dead works, and of faith toward God, of the doctrine of baptisms, and of laying on of hands, and of resurrection of the dead, and of eternal judgment" (Heb. 6:1–2). After that, I must lead them on to perfection through the more mature matters of holiness and the power of offering up our bodies as living sacrifices to God (Rom. 12:1–2; 1 Peter 1:15–16).

This millennium generation needs some Finneys, some Calvins, some Wesleys, and some Whitefields to cry in the wilderness until repentance sweeps across our land. We've had enough entertainment, and we've had enough professional pulpiteers. We need preachers who are determined to preach the pure doctrines of God's Word whether the people cheer and throw large offerings in the bucket.

We are reaping a whirlwind today because we do not teach sound doctrine to our children and our young people. Very few Christians hear sermons on doctrine anymore because we have replaced the authority of the local pastor and the local church with religious television superstars and entertainer preachers. Many of these elevated icons of politically correct preaching refuse to tell the whole truth of God's Word because doing that might shrink their crowds or—worst of all—dry up their offerings.

SHAKE US UP, LORD!

What we need is an outright revolution to shake us up and put us back on the right path. Remember, the prophet Isaiah proclaimed, "They that shall be of thee shall build the old waste places: thou shalt raise up the foundations of many generations; and thou shalt be called, The repairer of the breach, The restorer of paths to dwell in" (Isa. 58:12). Restorers restore things, and the Hebrew word translated "restore" is *shuwb*. It means "to turn back or return," "to start over again."[3]

The modern humanistic self-help gospel teaches us only to take care of our flesh, but that is the antithesis or opposite of the gospel of Jesus Christ. God spoke to me and said, "Look at this generation." In particular, I was to consider its young women. Anything that lives has several inherent properties: (1) it has appetite, (2) it has growth, (3) it has discharge, and (4) it possesses a burning desire to reproduce.

Young girls and women used to instinctively play with dolls and look forward to the day they could hold and care for their own babies. You may not realize it, but I am teaching Bible principles right now. Paul wrote, "I will therefore that the younger women marry, bear children, guide the house, give none occasion to the adversary to speak reproachfully" (1 Tim. 5:14). Paul also noted,

> The aged women likewise, that they be in behavior as becometh holiness, not false accusers, not given to much wine, teachers of good things; that they may teach the young women to be sober, to love their husbands, to love their children, to be discreet, chaste, keepers at home, good, obedient to their own husbands, that the word of God be not blasphemed. (Titus 2:3–5)

AREN'T WE SUPPOSED TO BE
THE INTELLIGENT CREATURES?

We are more career oriented than God oriented. We'll go along with God's Word as long as it won't hinder our careers and stop us from doing what we want to do. Babies are seen as hindrances in our society, which explains why so many young women claim it is their "right" to murder their young. Any species in nature that did the same would be wiped out in one to two generations! (And we are supposed to be the intelligent creatures made by God.)

When I asked the Lord what He was trying to tell me, He said, "The reason young women don't care anything about having children anymore is that they have become so self-interested." Then I understood. Normal women love their babies fiercely because they pay a high price to bring them into the world. They face the jaws of death to give life to their babies, and my wife has assured me that the road to delivery isn't pretty, quiet, or easy. This problem with the idolatry of self is just as bad, if not worse, among young men today. Everything is about us instead of the One who gave His life for us.

The apostle Paul and the apostles in Jerusalem faced a similar problem in their age. Notice how God dealt with "self" in the first-century church:

> And they continued steadfastly *in the apostles' doctrine* and fellowship, and in breaking of bread, and in prayers. And fear came upon every soul: and many wonders and signs were done by the apostles. (Acts 2:42–43, italics mine)

> Now I beseech you, brethren, mark them which cause divisions and offenses contrary to the doctrine which ye have learned; and avoid them. (Rom. 16:17)

> As I besought thee to abide still at Ephesus, when I went into Macedonia, that thou mightest charge some *that they teach no other doctrine,* neither give heed to fables and endless genealogies, which minister questions, rather than godly edifying which is in faith: so do. (1 Tim. 1:3–4, italics mine)

> Knowing this, that the law is not made for a righteous man, but for the lawless and disobedient, for the ungodly and for sinners,

for unholy and profane, for murderers of fathers and murderers of mothers, for manslayers, for whoremongers, for them that defile themselves with mankind, for menstealers, for liars, for per- jured persons, and if there be any other thing that is contrary to sound doctrine. (1 Tim. 1:9–10)

Those who openly and defiantly veered from sound Bible doc- trine were dealt with severely in the New Testament. Paul wrote, "Of whom is Hymenaeus and Alexander; whom I have delivered unto Satan, that they may learn not to blaspheme" (1 Tim. 1:20).

OUR GREATEST HOPE IS THE LOCAL PASTOR WHO PREACHES SOUND DOCTRINE

Earlier in this chapter, I mentioned the high percentages of homes I reach through my television broadcasts in the United States and Canada. Let me assure you that despite the apparent success, the Lord told me that national and international television programs like mine *are not the hope of America or of the world!* He made it clear that the hope of nations in the new millennium is the *local pastor* who preaches sound doctrine and faithfully leads a local church.

Paul reinforced this fact in his letter to Timothy: "But if I tarry long, that thou mayest know how thou oughtest to behave thyself in the house of God, which is the church of the living God, the pillar and ground of the truth" (1 Tim. 3:15). I didn't see anything about TV preachers being the "the pillar and ground of the truth." That privilege belongs exclusively to the church by God's command.

Christ-centered television programs may help the local church accomplish its vision, but nothing can take the place of the intimate and trusting relationship of a godly pastor with the members of his flock under God.

We need to get back to where we started. We need to fall in love with our Savior all over again. If His Word seems dry and lifeless to us, then we need to pray until God's Word becomes alive to us again. Part of our problem is that we have become too self-satisfied and self-sufficient. With our seminary training and packed traveling ministry schedule, we think we can do it all ourselves. I am afraid that many in the body of Christ are so backslidden that they can't tell the difference between the work of God and the work of man. Once we reach that point, we are in serious trouble: "Now the Spirit speaketh expressly, that in the latter times some shall depart from the faith, giving heed to seducing spirits, and doctrines of devils; speaking lies in hypocrisy; having their conscience seared with a hot iron" (1 Tim. 4:1–2).

WORDS OF FAITH AND GOOD DOCTRINE NOURISH OUR SOULS

Just because you are sincere doesn't mean you are right. You can be sincerely wrong (and if you don't know your doctrine, you probably are!). The apostle Paul told his young protégé about doctrine and the ministry: "If thou put the brethren in remembrance of these things, thou shalt be a good minister of Jesus Christ, nourished up *in the words of faith and of good doctrine,* whereunto thou hast attained" (1 Tim. 4:6, italics mine). Doctrine occupied a prominent place in Paul's instructions to Timothy:

> Till I come, give attendance to reading, to exhortation, to doctrine . . . Meditate upon these things; give thyself wholly to them; that thy profiting may appear to all. Take heed unto thyself, and unto the doctrine; continue in them: for in doing this thou shalt both save thyself, and them that hear thee. (1 Tim. 4:13, 15–16)

Let the elders that rule well be counted worthy of double honor, especially they who labor in the word and doctrine. (1 Tim. 5:17)

WHY DO WE NEED DOCTRINE TODAY?

Paul perfectly described our generation in his second letter to Timothy; then he reminded his student in the ministry how to preserve stability in the midst of chaos—it takes a godly life and example firmly rooted in the unchanging doctrines of the church of Jesus Christ:

> This know also, that in the last days perilous times shall come. For men shall be lovers of their own selves, covetous, boasters, proud, blasphemers, disobedient to parents, unthankful, unholy, without natural affection, trucebreakers, false accusers, incontinent, fierce, despisers of those that are good, traitors, heady, high-minded, lovers of pleasures more than lovers of God; having a form of godliness, but denying the power thereof: from such turn away. For of this sort are they which creep into houses, and lead captive silly women laden with sins, led away with divers lusts, ever learning, and never able to come to the knowledge of the truth. Now as Jannes and Jambres withstood Moses, so do these also resist the truth: men of corrupt minds, reprobate concerning the faith. But they shall proceed no further: for their folly shall be manifest unto all men, as theirs also was. But thou hast fully known *my doctrine, manner of life.* (2 Tim. 3:1–10, italics mine)

Paul clearly stated, "All scripture is given by inspiration of God, and is profitable for doctrine, for reproof, for correction, for instruction in righteousness" (2 Tim. 3:16). When was the last time you heard a solid message of reproof? How about a good rebuke?

OUR AGE EPITOMIZES THE "ITCHING EAR" GENERATION

We are living in an age that epitomizes the problem Paul predicted in his second letter to his young pastor friend:

> Preach the word; be instant in season, out of season; reprove, rebuke, exhort with all long-suffering and *doctrine*. For the time will come when they will not endure sound doctrine; but after their own lusts shall they heap to themselves teachers, having itching ears; and they shall turn away their ears from the truth, and shall be turned unto fables. (2 Tim. 4:2–4, italics mine)

This is why we must preach to the remnant instead of to the masses. We can't afford to be results driven. We have a mandate to say what God says and forget the rest:

> In all things showing thyself a pattern of good works: *in doctrine showing uncorruptness, gravity, sincerity,* sound speech, that cannot be condemned; that he that is of the contrary part may be ashamed, having no evil thing to say of you. Exhort servants to be obedient unto their own masters, and to please them well in all things; not answering again; not purloining, but showing all good fidelity; *that they may adorn the doctrine of God our Savior in all things*. For the grace of God that bringeth salvation hath appeared to all men, teaching us that, denying ungodliness and worldly lusts, we should live soberly, righteously, and godly, in this present world; looking for that blessed hope, and the glorious appearing

of the great God and our Savior Jesus Christ. (Titus 2:7–13, italics mine)

I AM SICK OF HUMANISTIC HOMILIES
AND PATTY-CAKE PABULUM

As a preacher, I am under commandment from God to preach sound doctrine, glorify Christ, and warn the wicked man of his wicked deeds, lest he continue in his wickedness and his blood be required at my hands. This nation has had enough humanistic homilies and patty-cake pabulum in the pulpits. It needs the saving power of the gospel of Christ.

The Lord asked me to spend all of the year 2000 preaching nothing but doctrine on national television and to my local congregation. I've preached on the baptism in the Holy Spirit on national television and prayed for people to be baptized in the Holy Spirit with the evidence of speaking in other tongues.

In the name of Jesus, I told homosexuals that they have a demon and they can be set free. Under the anointing of the Holy Spirit, I told millions of American television viewers that we don't need social reform, economic reform, or political reform. We need an old-fashioned, heaven-sent, Holy Spirit–filled, fire-baptized revival of righteousness and holy living. That will never happen unless God gives us preachers who will preach the timeless doctrines of the Bible come hell or high water.

We need revolutionary remnant preachers and believers who will boldly declare the biblical truths of baptisms, the second coming of Christ, and the power in Christ's blood. We need men and women who will declare the doctrines of our risen Lord with heaven's authority in their words, inspiration in their encouragement, and death in their stare.

God, give us a revolutionary remnant of believers who are

compelled by an inward desire to *serve an infallible Leader* with *irresistible power* based on *absolute truth.* If He gives us even a remnant tithe of the churchgoers in America, we will charge hell and snatch our nation out of the serpent's jaws!

CHAPTER 9

THE VIOLENT
TAKE IT BY FORCE

History tells us that most revolutions are violent and some-times bloody conflicts. Occasionally there have been bloodless coups in which one ruling party agrees to step down and relinquish control to another more powerful entity without a struggle.

God is not interested in a coup. This revolution is drenched in the blood of an innocent man, and it is the most violent of all revolutions. This revolution makes the bloody French Revolution pale in comparison because it is not limited to the realm of the flesh. It is a conflict of cosmic dimensions with eternal consequences.

Jesus said, "And from the days of John the Baptist until now the kingdom of heaven suffereth violence, and the violent take it by force" (Matt. 11:12). Only twenty-eight months later, Jesus died a bloody and tortured death, rose from the dead, and ascended on high. Then His disciples were endued with power by the Holy Spirit.

Peter the former denier became Peter the bold apostle, who preached the gospel of Jesus Christ to thousands of devout Jews in Jerusalem on the day of pentecost. Three thousand Jews received Christ as Lord and Savior that day, and the church was born with the very first explosion of Holy Spirit power through the medium of man (Acts 2).

The next thing we hear in the third chapter of the book of Acts, Peter and John paused long enough to give what they had to a disabled outcast positioned outside the Gate Beautiful. His excited response to his miraculous healing gathered another crowd to hear the second evangelistic sermon of the church. Five thousand souls pressed their way into the kingdom of light, and the apostles had the world's first megachurch after ministering only a week.

GOD POURED HIS POWER INTO FISHERMEN, MALCONTENTS, AND HOMEMAKERS

The steady stream of miracles, deliverance, and supernatural overthrow of the kingdom of darkness accelerated so quickly that the combined power of Rome and hell itself couldn't quench the revival fires. God poured His Holy Spirit power into fishermen, malcontents, doctors, lawyers, table waiters, and homemakers, and they turned their world upside down, epitomizing the true meaning of "no fear." It is amazing to see how fast things happen when people put Jesus at the center of their lives.

Revolution by one definition is "the overthrow or renunciation of one government or ruler and the substitution of another by the governed." It is also defined as "activity or movement designed to effect fundamental changes in the socioeconomic situation."[1]

In emergency rooms across the nation, cutting-edge trauma teams are using new lifesaving techniques perfected in the desperate operating theaters of the armed forces in times of war. When the patient's life hangs in the balance, emergency room physicians may violently strike the chest of a heart attack victim in a desperate attempt to trigger a heartbeat. If that fails, the doctor may actually straddle a man's body to crack open his rib cage. Then he will reach into the victim's chest cavity with his hands and massage the victim's heart back to life.

In the presence of life-threatening injuries or complications, medical trauma teams are trained to "major on the majors" and worry about the niceties of sutures and formal surgical protocols later! (Any doctor who performed such a procedure in the past may well have faced charges of assault and battery and attempted murder!)

Satan's seducing ways have landed America in God's emergency room with only moments to spare. Her heart has grown cold, and only drastic measures will do! The days of treating the symptoms and dressing the untreated wounds with greasy grace are over. It is time to crack open the encircling structures and lay hands on America's heart with loving violence and persistent resuscitation. It may take a village to raise a child, but it takes a cosmic revolution to overthrow the bondage of Satan and resurrect a nation.

DOCTOR CHURCH DISPENSED POWERLESS PLACEBOS

The nation stopped going to the doctor down the street long ago because Doctor Church dispensed powerless placebos and foolish fantasies instead of heavenly heart transplants. Religious nostrums and endless prescription programs didn't get the job done, and the popular practice of delivering carefully manicured and politically correct preaching only made things worse. Such spiritual malpractice has managed to inoculate the nation against the infectious power of genuine truth. This hell-bound generation doesn't need church as usual; it needs a preacher with a message steeped in heavenly violence and divine love.

A Holy Spirit invasion is taking place, and we need to lift up our voices like trumpets and sound the alarm. We need to realign the orbit of our lives to conform to the center of all things—the Son of the living God. Our Son is a burning fire and an eternal source of power and light. I am talking about putting God back on the throne at the center of our lives and ministries.

When we return the Son to the center of our universe, we will hear thousands of reports about miraculous healings occurring through Sister Susie's apron and Brother Mike's handkerchief. Holy Spirit–filled auto mechanics will lay hands on coworkers with limbs severed in the workplace and violently command them to be healed. And signs and wonders will become everyday occurrences.

IS YOUR SHADOW A VEHICLE OF HEALING POWER?

Average shopping days will become community healing days when the shadows of the saints become vehicles of the healing power of the Holy Spirit in shopping malls, grocery stores, car lots, and Saturday morning yard sales. It is time for every table waiter in the kingdom to step out into the streets of cities and towns with the "Stephen anointing" to pray the prayer of faith for the sick and dying. As the Lord declared through the prophet thousands of years ago, "Behold, I will do a *new thing;* now it shall spring forth; shall ye not know it? I will even make a way in the wilderness, and rivers in the desert" (Isa. 43:19, italics mine).

If we ever get the church back into the center of God's purposes, we will see nations born in a day. We will see new God-centered television and Internet networks explode on the expanse of America's landscape so rapidly that it will stagger the imagination. An unprecedented transfer of wealth will shift the economic balance of power into the hands of the redeemed at the speed of light, exactly as it happened in Egypt thousands of years ago when Moses led God's people out of bondage after the first Passover. Demons will tremble every time a violent remnant saint comes into view, and the pig population of the world will suffer unprecedented losses for inexplicable reasons![2]

I am a man possessed by the Spirit of God. It is time for a violent overthrow in the heavenlies and a total revolution among men. We need to pray and preach as we have never done before. We should be laying our hands on everyone we can touch in the name of Jesus. We hold the key to set our nation and the world free.

Do you believe in the impartation of spiritual genealogy? God does. We see it in the impartation of a double anointing upon Elisha (he received Elijah's mantle of anointing on top of his own). Moses imparted his anointing to Joshua just before his death (earlier, he had imparted a measure of his anointing to the seventy judges appointed at Jethro's recommendation). Evidently Samuel imparted a measure of his prophetic anointing to young David as well. We have no record of him prophesying until after the aged prophet anointed him.

TIMOTHY GOT IT BY "THE PUTTING ON OF HANDS"

Jesus breathed upon His disciples, and the apostle Paul laid his hands upon young Timothy to impart a spiritual gift. He wrote, "Wherefore I put thee in remembrance that thou stir up the gift of God, which is in thee by the putting on of my hands" (2 Tim. 1:6).

When we pray for the lost, the sick, the dying, the discouraged, and the demonized in the coming days, we will not be alone. Our spiritual heritage will be there with us. Paul wasn't filling space with empty eloquence when he said we are "compassed about with so great a cloud of witnesses" (Heb. 12:1).

I know that I know that when I pray for the thousands of people who attend our meetings around the country, the God-given anointing and apostolic mantles of Dr. Lester Sumrall, Smith Wigglesworth, Howard Carter, and Aimee Semple McPherson flow through me as I minister in Jesus' name.

How can I say such a thing? I have submitted myself to their godly instruction and correction in person or in the Spirit through their teachings and example. It is time for us to stand up and be heard as representatives of Jesus Christ and all of those who have gone before us in the faith. That sets in motion the timeless transfer of faith and power through the Holy Spirit to violently overthrow every demonic stronghold and shed Christ's light into every pit of darkness.

WE'VE BACKED UP AND LAIN LOW LONG ENOUGH!

We are destined to wreck Satan's house and overthrow his filthy playpen through the irresistible power of the Holy Spirit. Violent overthrow comes only when the dialogue between two opposing interests comes to its apex of limitation. The time is now; negotiation can no longer be tolerated. We have backed up, hunkered down, held our tongues, and lain low long enough.

We have reached a strategic inflection point, and a decision must be made. If God be God, then we must serve Him without reservation or hesitation. It is time for the church to rise up and tell the forces of hell where to go! Without a revolution, the diluted church of the lukewarm and the frozen wouldn't dare defy the denizens of darkness.

The modern church already knows what it is like to proclaim a powerless gospel in the name of One it barely knows. A Christendom that adheres to the doctrine of spiritual passivity must be well acquainted with the humiliation of defeat at the hands of its defeated foe who leaves it naked, wounded, and despised in the eyes of the world.

Once again we return to the words of the King of kings and Lord of lords, the One who suffered unspeakable violence on our behalf.

The One called both Lamb and Lion said, "And from the days of John the Baptist until now *the kingdom of heaven suffereth violence, and the violent take it by force*" (Matt. 11:12, italics mine). The kingdom of heaven will never be "taken" by a hostile force. Luke the physician illuminated this truth in his gospel when he wrote, "The law and the prophets were until John: since that time the kingdom of God is preached, *and every man presseth into it*" (Luke 16:16, italics mine).

GOD'S KINGDOM IS DESTINED TO BE IMPOSED WHERE IT IS NOT WELCOME

By the terms *kingdom of heaven* and *kingdom of God,* we refer to "anywhere the rule of God is *imposed.*" Notice that I did *not* say it is where the rule of God is "enforced." There is a world of difference between enforcement and imposition. God's kingdom is destined to be imposed where it is not welcome.

You enforce a thing by requiring obedience to a set of standards, limitations, or requirements *agreed upon* by a society or government. Our authority goes far beyond enforcement and into the realm of imposition. We have a mandate to *impose* the rule of God over every spirit in existence and, where necessary, over every human being influenced by rebellious spirits. Jesus did not lay down His life to preserve our right to vote on the rules of the kingdom and then elect someone to enforce them. That is the way of man's religion: "Wear your dress this far from the knee. Do your hair this way, or the religious elite hall monitor wearing the extraholy outfit will get you."

God has the right to impose His order on His creation: "For the earth is the Lord's, and the fullness thereof" (1 Cor. 10:26). Everything belongs to Him, including your mind, your body, your future, your past, your relationships, and your church. He is about to impose His kingdom on the earth, and I sense the beginnings of a violent overthrow, upheaval, and revolution.

It is inevitable. This isn't a question of earthly governments in disagreement. The conflict involves hidden powers and spirit kingdoms, not mere earthly structures. The apostle Paul's battle strategies still stand true as we face a spiritual conflict of global proportions:

> Put on the whole armor of God, that ye may be able to stand against the wiles of the devil. For we wrestle not against flesh and blood, but against principalities, against powers, against the rulers of the darkness of this world, against spiritual wickedness in high places. Wherefore take unto you the whole armor of God, that ye may be able to withstand in the evil day, and having done all, to stand. (Eph. 6:11–13)

SATAN DOES NOT FEAR WHIMPERED PRAYERS UTTERED IN DOUBT AND UNBELIEF

Satan is a defeated foe, but he will continue to wreak havoc in our world as long as God's people hide their light, muffle their voices, compromise their convictions, and whimper their prayers toward heaven from hearts encumbered by doubt and unbelief.

Jesus Christ will not come back for less than He left. We need to know the answer when someone asks us, "Are you a Christian?" while holding a 12-gauge shotgun or an Uzi submachine gun. Are we fakes, or do we really possess something money can't buy and humanity can't produce?

I perceive a rumbling and a shaking proceeding from a royal remnant who will gladly expend their lives for a cause they believe greater than their very lives. I previously stated this unforgettable quote adapted from statements made by the late Will Durant, but I want to say it again:

> There's no greater drama than a few remnant preachers scorned by a succession of adversaries, bearing trials with tenacity, multiplying miraculously, building order in chaos, all the while rescuing the despondent, redeeming the downtrodden, and reviving the life of Christ in the hearts of humanity. Oh they're beaten and battered, but they are not bowed.

These believers are propelled by a power that is greater than themselves. They are compelled by an inward desire to serve an infallible Leader with irresistible power based on absolute truth!

IT'S TIME FOR THE SICKLE AND THE REAPER, NOT THE DOUBTERS AND POUTERS

The time has come for the risen Son to lead us into battle. The alarm is heard, and it is time to strap on our armor and go to war. The fields are white, and this is the time for the sickle and the reaper, not the doubters and pouters. Let the revolution begin with a shout, not a whimper. We are about to invade enemy-held territory, and we've been empowered to win.

We take the example of Jesus as our model for conquest. Jesus didn't beg, weep, and cry over blind Bartimeus. He forgave the man's sins (without bothering to ask the permission of the Pharisees or Sadducees) and said, "Go thy way; thy faith hath made thee whole" (Mark 10:52).

Jesus raised Lazarus from the dead, even though He probably knew it would be the last straw for the priests and Pharisees. They were so angry that they plotted to kill Jesus *and* Lazarus! (See John 11:46–53; 12:10–11.) Why? Jesus Christ *imposed* the kingdom over every elaborate man-centered religious and political kingdom, with or without the approval of Jerusalem and Rome. The Lord even imposed it upon prostitutes, thieves, and a weak, timid man warming himself by the fire of the world while denying His name.

As the revolutionary remnant people move closer and closer to the Son, everything speeds up and heats up at an exponential rate. The first-century disciples were close to Him, and they saw the church born in a day. All of Asia Minor heard the gospel in only two years and three months in a day when automobiles, telephones, and printing presses did not exist.

TIME IS COLLAPSING ON ITSELF

In this revolution, we will accomplish in ten minutes what used to take ten years. We will produce in a matter of days, weeks, or months what used to require a lifetime of labor. We will reap where we did not sow because time is collapsing on itself. Through the power of God almighty, we will give one command, and a million souls will be swept into His kingdom. One mighty shout, "Come out of them, you unclean spirit!" will trigger the instantaneous deliverance of one hundred thousand homosexuals and lesbians!

This revolution will "effect fundamental changes in the socioeconomic situation" of our world. We can no longer sit in our churches and sing "Amazing Grace," fold our hands, and hope the world gets saved. We cannot afford to sing, "This is the day that the Lord hath made," while avoiding or stepping over the downcast and hurting humanity He has empowered us to deliver.

God doesn't want a kingdom of blood-washed Pharisees who carefully avoid and shun the social and spiritual "lepers and outcasts" outside our gilded gates while we go about our religious exercises within. God gave us power to *impose* His kingdom in the earth, not to *enclose* His kingdom and separate ourselves from the lost.

AN UNLIKELY CROWD WILL PRESS ITS WAY INTO GOD'S KINGDOM

The hurting and the hungry will press their way into God's kingdom with violence just as the redeemed remnant violently imposes God's kingdom and rule upon the dark realm of Satan. We will see an unlikely crowd press its way into God's kingdom, and it is certainly not the kind of people we would have chosen.

The new breed of ragged remnants won't look right, dress right, smell right, or talk right, but they belong to Him. They won't speak or understand our Christianese dialect and culture because these new believers didn't grow up in the church; they grew up in the world among thieves, murderers, harlots, and publicans.

Can I tell you something? God has an entire army of unborn people in this land, and you won't find them lounging around in our padded church auditoriums. They are sitting on bar stools and shooting heroin into their veins; nonetheless, they are His, and He is going to have them.

They are not sitting on a church pew; they are busy selling their bodies for twenty dollars a customer. But they belong to Another, and He is going to have them. They may be sitting in the governor's mansion with a loaded pistol in their hands and a suicide note in their briefcase, but it is not their time yet. They belong to the King, and He is going to have them.

Are we ready for the harvest that is coming? Fishermen in slow seasons can easily become fish sorters who like to pick and choose from their meager catch each day. When we return to our first love and draw closer to the Son, we won't have time for fish sorting because there is something about intimacy and obedience to Jesus that produces net-breaking harvests.

Jesus has called us to become fishers of men. In the coming harvest, the souls of men will come into the gospel net so fast and furiously that we won't be able to analyze and quantify them through our antiquated religious sifting systems.

THIS REVOLUTION HAS A MUCH GREATER SYMBOL OF REMEMBRANCE

In 1886, the patriots who fought through the American Revolution and the War of 1812 were honored by a gift from France called the Statue of Liberty. This copper statue stands on Liberty Island in New York Harbor with an inscription that reads, "Give me your tired, your poor, your huddled masses yearning to breathe free." Now we embark on a much greater revolution with a much greater symbol of remembrance. Two nail-scarred hands are extended and a divine invitation goes out to all humanity: "Come unto me, all ye that labor and are heavy laden, and I will give you rest" (Matt. 11:28).

When we begin to invade Satan's hunting grounds and take back what belongs to us, we can be sure we will have a fight on our hands. Victory is assured if we fight the good fight and hold to the faith.

Paul wrote his final letter to Timothy from a darkened Roman dungeon receiving a small shaft of light from a hole in the ceiling. He had to move toward the light so his aged hands could write to young Timothy. Perhaps a Roman soldier peered through that hole and noticed that the great apostle's tunic had fallen from around his shoulders. "Sir," he gasped, "what heinous and vicious crime have you committed?" "Why do you ask that?" "The scars upon your back, sir, are reserved for the most heinous and vicious criminals." "Don't mind those," said Paul. "They are just the scars of battle. You see, I've come to rout the enemy. I have been ship-wrecked, snakebitten, stoned and left for dead, but I count it all joy. Don't mind those, lad; they are just the trophies of battle. Soon I will have fought the good fight and will have kept the faith. Therefore there is a crown laid up for me and not for me only, but for all those who love His appearing."

The path of the righteous grows brighter and brighter, and the violent revolutionary remnant is on the march. Today is the day of victory. This is the day the Lord has made, and this is the day we make our stand in His name. It is time for violence in the kingdom of light; there are kingdoms and realms to conquer and millions of souls to set free in the King's name.

We have orders to serve notice on Satan that we've come to claim God's property and press them into the kingdom. We have the authority to use deadly force if he resists. Billions of people are going to hell, and it is our job to stop them.

We have a commission to impose God's kingdom on the king-dom of darkness. That means we have power and authority through God's Word to break every chain and loose every captive in Jesus' name. God purposely let Satan draw first blood on a lonely tree in Jerusalem, but that blood has become our healing flow and redeem-ing flood. Once the harvest is brought in, a much greater event is scheduled to occur.

CHAPTER 10

GET RIGHT
OR GET LEFT

We have much to gain by a return to the discarded values of the past, and we have much to lose if we do not. Something strange happened to me while preaching to ten thousand people in a major auditorium in a large city. It shook my life more than any other incident in nearly a quarter of a century of preaching and ministry.

My message began with one of the most familiar and beloved passages in the New Testament—a scripture from the gospel penned by John the Beloved under the inspiration of God:

> Let not your heart be troubled: ye believe in God, believe also in me. In my Father's house are many mansions: if it were not so, I would have told you. I go to prepare a place for you. And if I go and prepare a place for you, I will come again, and receive you unto myself; that where I am, there ye may be also. (John 14:1–3)

Everybody shouted, danced, and ran up and down the aisles . . . until I began to preach about what Jesus meant by those words. Since I believe we should always try to interpret God's Word using other related passages in the Scriptures, I quoted and expounded on Jesus' statements about the coming of the Son of man in the gospels of Matthew and Luke.

I reminded the people that the Lord said, "Then shall two be in the field; the one shall be taken, and the other left" (Matt. 24:40). Then we moved to the next two verses in expository fashion: "Two women shall be grinding at the mill; the one shall be taken, and the other left. Watch therefore: for ye know not what hour your Lord doth come" (Matt. 24:41–42).

THEN I BEGAN TO PREACH ABOUT HEAVEN

Following the Lord's example in the Gospels, I began to preach about a place called heaven. Evoking the image of the older saints in the kingdom, I described how their physical bodies have begun to wind down and their raven black hair or brilliant red locks have turned white or silvery gray. "There are many senior saints among us whose skin is no longer taut on their faces," I said, "but there will come a time when they will leap like harts over the everlasting hills of God to suffer no more, to cry no more, to sigh no more, and to die no more!"

Then it happened.

As soon as I began to preach about what the Bible calls "the blessed hope," thousands of blood-washed Christians in that auditorium summarily cut me off![1] The shouting was over. The dancing had turned to stamping. Instead of running for joy, they slumped in their seats and searched their pockets and sorted through their purses for breath mints.

That crowd wouldn't listen to me preach. They made it clear that they didn't want to hear anything about heaven, and they especially didn't want to hear me talk about a rapture. They preferred to listen to preachers of the new millennium who were gifted in the art of avoiding the politically incorrect subject of sin.

How could such a thing happen in a Christian conference hosted by leading men of God whom I deeply respect? First, most of the people came to that regional conference from other places and did not attend the churches served by those solid men of God.

THEY FEASTED ON A SOUL-FATTENING SELF-HELP GOSPEL

Second, and most important, most of those people (and most American Christians in general) have feasted for twenty years on the soul-fattening fare of a self-help humanist gospel. Their spiritual "meat" was anchored in the temporality of this present world. In the real world, it means the "me right now" world.

This is the religion preached and propagated by the blame shifters we discussed earlier in this book. It can cater to the "poor old me, I am a lifetime victim" people. On the other hand, it can also press the hot buttons of the masses by openly focusing on the "me" issues: *my* house, *my* spiritual gifts, *my* children, *my* marriage, *my* life, *my* goals, *my* place in the sun.

A nationally known television preacher stopped me after that meeting and asked, "You don't really *believe* that, do you?" I looked at him and responded, "Believe what?" He said, "Well, do you mean that you still believe there is a literal city built foursquare? Do you actually believe that there is a throne established of God and that out of that throne proceeds a river? And do you believe that on either side of that river there are twelve manners of fruit and the leaves of those trees are for the healing of the nations? Do you actually believe in streets of gold?"

If you don't know my answer to his questions, let me share it with you: *of course I believe what the Bible says about heaven! Don't you?*[2]

I have many godly friends in the ministry who differ with me when it comes to the end times. That is fine with me because I know these ministers love the Lord Jesus and view the Bible as holy Writ, not holy opinion. This particular gentleman disagreed with me as well, but he was not one of those friends who believed the Bible from cover to cover.

WHO ARE WE TO EDIT GOD'S WORD FOR PERSONAL CONVENIENCE?

Regardless of our personal opinions about the end times, we should all agree on the divine inspiration and unequivocal authority of God's Word. No one—and I mean *no one*—walking this earth on two legs has the divine wisdom, divine understanding, or divine authority to take a pair of scissors or a wide-tipped black marker to God's Word to edit it for the sake of convenience or pet human theories. I say that because *that is what it takes to discount the words of Jesus quoted in detail by multiple eyewitnesses.*

After that meeting, I asked God in prayer, "Lord, what is going on?" His answer unsettled me. He said, "They have replaced the preacher and My Word with something else. Many churches have moved the preaching pulpit from the center to the side."

Ignorance is the inevitable result of the displacement of God's Word from the center of our faith. We won't know anything about God if we refuse to study and heed what He says about Himself in His Book of Remembrance.

Even sincere worship that is not guided by God's spoken desires and instructions can become unacceptable and sinful in God's eyes. If you don't believe me, then consider the folly of Cain; and study the fatal failure of King David the first time he tried to return the ark of the covenant to Jerusalem. Only after David returned to the discarded values of Moses and the guiding

Scriptures from God was he able to safely return God's presence to the royal city. (See 1 Chron. 13:6–14; 15:1–2, 12–16.)

THERE IS PRECIOUS LITTLE LEFT TO BALANCE OUR BIBLE-IMPAIRED PULPITS

My chief concern in this chapter is the widespread disregard of many Christians for central tenets of our faith. Many who call Jesus their Lord somehow feel free to toss out or explain away every statement He and His prophets made about heaven, hell, sin, the catching away of the saints, His second coming, the Great Tribulation, and the Final Judgment! (There is little else left to bring balance to the endless flesh petting and ego pampering that proceed from our Bible-impaired pulpits!)

One prominent doctrine in vogue today claims that the statements Jesus made in John 14 about the many mansions in His Father's house don't really refer to a literal heaven. Teachers in this camp say, "Heaven is figurative because we can't understand God. Whatever God is, that is what we're going to become. Since we don't really know what He is, then there are really no streets of gold or mansions waiting for us."

I confess that at times I get angry over what is going on. I feel a righteous anger rise up when I realize that most of the body of Christ today know more about Luke 6:38 than they do about John 3:16. I get upset when I see someone stealing the blessed hope from God's people in the name of wisdom. Too many Christians in this generation give up and quit if they don't get their headache healed when a man of God lays hands on them. Count on the fact that you and I are going to have some hard times in this life. Anyone who presumes to tell you otherwise is a liar, plain and simple. He is trying to contradict the Word of God, which tells us, "All that will live godly in Christ Jesus shall suffer persecution" (2 Tim. 3:12).

HOPE IS A DIVINE STRENGTH THAT
ABIDES WITH THE HUMAN SOUL

Let me repeat these words of Jesus one more time: "Let not your heart be troubled: ye believe in God, believe also in me. In my Father's house are many mansions" (John 14:1–2). We have become so eccentrically self-interested and preoccupied with our present that we have denied ourselves the help available through a godly hope for the future. Hope is a divine strength that abides with the human soul and causes it to have a deep, inner knowing that tomorrow may be better than today.

A great deal of preaching generally discounts the idea of the catching away of the saints before or during a great tribulation in the earth. The central focus of these teachings is the quest to fix up this earth so that we can live here and prepare it for Christ so He can return and join us.

Well, I really don't want to take over this planet when I compare it to what I can have as an inheritance from my heavenly Father. You can have every inch of the Okefenokee Swamps in Florida or the Grand Canyon, but I want to gaze into the eyes of my Creator and caress the wounded hands of my Redeemer. You can have all of the gold on this planet if you want it, but I will be content to pass through the golden gates of that celestial city and walk down those streets of gold in an eternal morning with His praises on my lips.

In all fairness, many of my friends who have problems with the Rapture are reacting to the extreme teachings and shortsighted actions of Christians who focus so exclusively on the "catching away of the saints" that they stop trying to win the lost or minister to the poor and needy. Some of these people have charged their credit cards to the limit and walked away from their homes (and their mounting delinquent mortgage payments) to hide out in caves "until Jesus comes." This is every bit as wrong as trying to dismiss the clear declarations of Jesus Christ about heaven, hell, His sudden return, and the Judgment.

WE SHOULD LIVE HOLY
AND BUILD TO LAST ANOTHER MILLENNIUM

I believe in the imminent or soon return of our Lord, but I also believe that no man can predict or know the day of His sudden return. I believe we should live holy lives as if He will return with our next breath, but we should also obey the Lord's command that we occupy until His return. That means you build the things God tells you to build as if they will have to last a thousand years or a thousand generations. That means you devote all of your energies to obeying the Word of God, bringing in the great harvest, and discipling the next generation of revolutionary remnant leaders. That means you lay everything you are and everything you hope to be at the feet of Jesus; and then you take up your cross without hesitation or comment like a good soldier.

Despite their great potential for occasional oddities, I love people on both extremes—as long as they love and obey the Lord Jesus Christ more than anything else (including their opinions about the beginning and the end of time and anything else in between).

My friends of the "no Rapture" persuasion enjoy my preaching because they know they can shout and rejoice when I preach what the Bible says about the day we will become a glorious church without spot or wrinkle. They stand to their feet when I preach the Bible truth that it is our duty to occupy the land in the supreme power and authority of the Lord of lords and King of kings until He returns.

My friends who preach the Rapture love to have me visit their churches too. I preach the *same message* everywhere I go, but these brothers and sisters shout and praise God when I preach about the mansions Jesus has prepared for us in His Father's house. They can hardly wait until we turn to the many scriptures describing the moment He will return for His blood-washed people.

THE WORLD IS BUT A DRESSING ROOM
WHERE WE PUT ON IMMORTALITY

The Scriptures picture this world as a staging room, a dressing room where we will put on immortality before embarking on a greater journey with the Creator. What we do here *does* matter, but we need to continually view things through a heavenly perspective. That doesn't encourage us to discard this life as if it doesn't matter; it exhorts us to live, act, and minister *as if God is watching* (which He is).

When we allow someone to steal away the blessed hope God gave us, we lose hope itself. There is a *good reason* for God's balancing our lives between the urgency of the present and the eternity of the future. We need both anchors in our lives.

God is our Rock and Shield, and our ever-present hope in this life; but He is also our blessed hope for the life to come. James the apostle wrote,

> For what is your life? It is even a vapor, that appeareth for a little time, and then vanisheth away. For that ye ought to say, If the Lord will, we shall live, and do this, or that. But now ye rejoice in your boastings: all such rejoicing is evil. (James 4:14–16)

GOD IS DISPLEASED IF WE DISCOUNT EITHER
THIS LIFE OR THE LIFE TO COME

This earthly life is a gift to be stewarded carefully, but eternal life in Christ is an infinitesimally greater gift of immeasurable worth. God is displeased when we discount either gift.

One of the great benefits of our blessed hope in Jesus' return is that when all else fails, hope will join with faith to carry us through the pain and agony of cancer. Your blessed hope and conviction that there is more to life than *this temporary existence* will help you get through the valley if your spouse walks out on you and slams the door. I'm sorry, but I prefer to deal with the realities of life's challenges and God's genuine answers for them.

I've prayed for hundreds of thousands of desperately sick people over the last two decades, and many of them have been raised up and miraculously healed by the power of God. I believe in the prayer of faith, the power of the blood, and the healing virtue in Jesus' stripes. However, there are times when for reasons unknown to man, the sick remain sick, and the dying continue their steady journey toward death.

I refuse to push all of those people into a box and say, "They didn't get healed because they didn't have faith." Nor will I ever say that God does not answer prayer or work miracles today. The truth is that we don't know everything! That is one of the reasons God gave us a blessed hope.

THEY LOOKED DEATH IN THE FACE AND STOOD ON THEIR BLESSED HOPE

Martyrs who look death in the face and declare that Jesus is Lord look toward a blessed hope of resurrection, not merely a distant reformation of their persecutors. If you don't have a dollar to your name and your body is wracked with pain despite all that you can do, you still have this blessed hope that someday . . .

If I'm looking only for help in the natural arena, then I don't need the gospel. However, if I want hope to carry me beyond the scope of human limitation, then I have to look beyond the natural and into the supernatural. I must step into the realm where I believe God meant what He said and said what He meant in His Word.

Frankly if God said in the Gospels or the Prophets that in heaven we will wear pink pajamas and polka-dotted underwear, then I want you to know that I want my own personal set! I am setting fires of holy revolution and blazing trails of conquest in this life, but my eyes are also fixed on a blessed realm the Bible calls heaven. That is where I am going. What about you?

Sometimes I cry out, "God, please help this hell-bound generation! Awaken this church that has been lulled to sleep and deprived of the blessed hope, Lord." For several years leading up to our new millennium, there was a great dividing in the church. The Lord already seems to be separating the sheep from the goats in His flock. You may feel an alarm going off because you didn't realize that not everyone who sits in a church pew is ready for the Lord's return.

God knows what He is doing, but most of us do not. He told us in plain, everyday terms (whether we want to read it in Greek, Hebrew, Aramaic, English, German, or Hindi) that He is coming "in an hour when you think not." Now why would God say a thing like that? He said it (and He will do it) because *He wants us to live ready.* When He comes, it will be at the speed of light; people around the globe will stand amazed at the magnificent magnitude of His perfection as His heavenly band sweeps through our world from north to south. If you think I am waxing eloquent in this text, look up some of these Bible references and consider the Lord's words for yourself:

1. He will come in glory and reward every man (Matt. 16:27).

2. He will come as a thief in the night (1 Thess. 5:2–3).

3. He will come as the lightning out of the east (Matt. 24:27).

4. All the tribes of earth will see Him (Matt. 24:29–31, 36).

5. Watch for the hour of His coming (Matt. 24:37–42).

6. You will see Him coming in the clouds of heaven (Matt. 26:64).

7. When these things begin to come to pass, look up (Luke 21:24–28).

8. He will come with all His saints (1 Thess. 3:13).

9. Be patient, for His coming is getting closer (James 5:7–8).

10. Those in their graves shall hear His voice and arise (John 5:28–29).

11. There will be no more tears, death, sorrow, or pain, but there will be a lake of fire (Rev. 21:4–8).

12. Then the end shall come (Matt. 24:14, 21–22).

WHERE IS THE PROMISE OF HIS COMING? RIGHT HERE

Be mindful of the words which were spoken before by the holy prophets, and of the commandment of us the apostles of the Lord and Savior: knowing this first, that there shall come in the last days scoffers, walking after their own lusts, and saying, *Where is the promise of his coming?* for since the fathers fell asleep, all things continue as they were from the beginning of the creation. For this *they willingly are ignorant of* . . . But, beloved, be not ignorant of this one thing, that one day is with the Lord as a thousand years, and a thousand years as one day . . . But the day of the Lord will come as a thief in the night. (2 Peter 3:2–5, 8, 10, italics mine)

It is time to toe the line and be counted as members of God's divinely energized and directed revolutionary force. In due time, our Captain will appear in the heavens on a white horse to finish what He started before the beginning of time. In my Bible, John described His appearance and said it caused him to fall to the ground as though he were dead.

> His head and his hairs were white like wool, as white as snow; and his eyes were as a flame of fire; and his feet like unto fine brass, as if they burned in a furnace; and his voice as the sound of many waters. And he had in his right hand seven stars: and out of his mouth went a sharp two-edged sword: and his countenance was as the sun shineth in his strength. (Rev. 1:14–16)

This celestial Captain with eyes of flame is looking for more remnant believers like John the apostle. Men like John are not born; they are built by their battles. Their character is formed by their failures and promoted by their persecution. Dr. Martin Luther King Jr. said the true measure of such a man is not how he stands in times of comfort or convenience but how he stands in times of challenge and controversy. This is a day for us to stand and be counted. It is time for us to get right or get left!

The same Jesus who said, "Lift up your eyes, and look on the fields; for they are white already to harvest" (John 4:35), told us He was going to prepare a place for us in His Father's house. People who want to preach that there isn't a literal heaven are laughable to me, regardless of the degrees or impressive titles in front of or after their names. If they don't believe that Jesus said what He meant and meant what He said, then they have disqualified themselves from having any say in the matter of God's kingdom.

If you serve the King, then you listen to and obey His commands. If you don't, then you aren't part of His kingdom. (I didn't say that—the King of kings said it in John 14:23–24.)

Let me seal this chapter with a comment from an informed and authoritative source about religious ignorance:

I would not have you to be ignorant, brethren, concerning them which are asleep, that ye sorrow not, *even as others which have no hope*. For if we believe that Jesus died and rose again, even so them also which sleep in Jesus will God bring with him. For this we say unto you by the word of the Lord, that we which are alive and remain unto the coming of the Lord shall not prevent them which are asleep. *For the Lord himself shall descend from heaven with a shout, with the voice of the archangel, and with the trump of God:* and the dead in Christ shall rise first: *then we which are alive and remain shall be caught up together with them in the clouds, to meet the Lord in the air:* and so shall we ever be with the Lord. Wherefore comfort one another with these words. (1 Thess. 4:13–18, italics mine)

Paul the apostle of faith was talking about the Rapture. I don't mean to startle anyone, but this is a central doctrine of the New Testament church and the unchangeable Word of God. It demands a verdict and actions to match.

CHAPTER 11

WE NEED TO HEAR
MOTHERS PRAY!

Never underestimate the power of a mother's travailing prayer.[1] This force unleashes immeasurable divine power that can salvage even the worst of prodigals seconds before their souls would plunge irretrievably into the eternal nightmare of hell's abyss. I have vivid memories of the day I first discovered this well of power in 1964.

Lyndon B. Johnson was the president of the United States, and I entered the second grade that year. I was never without my six-shooter cap pistols (except in church—every respectable sheriff removes all cap guns and his hat in the house of God) or my constant companion, Lady. She was a big collie that was as tall as I was and did double duty as my "horse."

As a "professional boy," I had the duty to be a boy to the bone. You couldn't get me to even touch a Barbie doll (let alone a Ken doll), and if I wasn't dirty, something was wrong with me. I remember wondering if the other kids' legs looked like mine—black and blue from my toes to my hips. (Of course, I didn't worry about what they looked like because I refused to wear sissy short pants. My preferred wardrobe consisted of Wrangler jeans, cowboy boots, and a T-shirt.)

I considered myself the sheriff of the entire south end of Columbus, Ohio, and I made my headquarters just off Frank Road in our family home. I remember being at peace, and I don't remember having nightmares. The most violent thing I can remember was the time Tonto fell off his horse on the *Lone Ranger*. There weren't any video games or arcades back then, but I was happy as long as I had my stick pony.

THE SWEEPER WAS RUNNING WITH
NO ONE AT THE CONTROLS!

With that background, you will understand me when I say there had been lots of shooting and some rough riding out on the range that day (weary old Lady just wasn't cooperating). I took a break from crime fighting to run into our wood-frame house for a drink. When I heard the sound of the vacuum cleaner upstairs, I clomped up the stairs in my well-worn cowboy boots to check on Mama. Rounding the corner, I stopped suddenly to consider the situation. The vacuum sweeper was running, but no one was at the controls! To be honest with you, my first thought as a churchgoing second grader was, "Mama's gone in the Rapture, and I've been left behind."

I remembered what the preachers said about "two in the bed, one taken and one left." I remembered the part about "two at the mill grinding, one taken and one left," but I'm not sure I knew what a mill was. My favorite part was the talk about our time and how airplanes would veer off their courses and driverless cars would drive off the road. Even with all of that, I wasn't prepared for the day I came upstairs and found the sweeper running in the middle of our hallway all alone.

When I ran over to the sweeper, I heard somebody crying in a bedroom. Then I heard the person pounding on the floor, and I couldn't resist investigating further. I cautiously opened the door and looked around the room, but once again, no one was there. Then I saw the shoes thrown on the floor, and I knew someone had made a place for herself in the closet. The only thing left to do was check the clothes closet. I moved closer to the closet, cracked open the door, and released a silent sigh of relief. It was Mama. She was down on her knees praying while still wearing her apron.

She had been apprehended by something far stronger and more urgent than sweeping the floors. While she went about her business of the day as a wife and mother, a long arm from another world apprehended her and led her into that closet of prayer. That is where I found Mama in a pool of tears. I had never heard her cry out to God as she did that day. She wasn't asking for a new sweeper or a new Sunday dress. She wasn't asking for a new house or for prosperity for the family.

DO WHATEVER YOU HAVE TO DO, GOD! SAVE MY CHILDREN!

I'll never forget hearing Mama cry out, "God, save my babies! Don't let Rodney and Debbie live and die and go to hell. O Lord, send an angel across their path. Whatever they are doing, stop them and make Yourself real to them! If You have to have an angel show up in their bedroom, please do whatever You have to do, God. Save my children!"

Christian parents across America have teenagers in their homes wearing long black coats and nose and tongue rings. They put black polish on their fingernails, white makeup on their faces, and black or bloodred highlights underneath and above their eyes. They hide *Playboy* magazines underneath their mattresses and display an Internet bomb-building site on their computer monitors. Meanwhile, all their parents can find time to do is to slip into a Sunday morning service every now and then. They'll get angry if the choir doesn't sing just right or if the preacher's message strikes a bit too close for comfort. But through it all, they never seem to find a way to their prayer closet.

If you just read a description of your home situation or if you are mad because the elders in your church can't do anything with your seventeen-year-old, you probably realize that you waited too long. You should have found yourself a prayer closet when that teenager was in the second grade, but you didn't. You could have avoided a lot of pain if your child had grown up with a vivid memory of Mama gripping the horns of the altar of God with superhuman strength while she called the forces of heaven down to earth on the child's behalf.

What now? Pray. Pray as you've never prayed before! Find that old closet and toss out enough of those shoes and clothing boxes to make yourself a secret place of prayer. Grip the horns of the altar of God in Jesus' name and ask the Lord to dispatch the angels of heaven on your child's behalf. It is *late,* but if your child is still alive, it isn't *too* late!

WE DON'T KNOW HOW TO PRAY ANYMORE

For too many of us, prayer consists of a mumbled concoction of religious rudiments we picked up somewhere. We'll mouth a "name it-claim it, blab it-grab it" prayer confession and then go on because we have to get our hair done or change the oil in the car. "Sorry, God, but we have to get to Little League, bowling league, and in-between league." The truth is that some of us don't know where our children are most of the time, yet we are quick to point our fingers at all of the evil things "causing" their fall from truth.

Frankly I'm tired of hearing parents blame the Internet, Hollywood, and the gun laws for their parenting problems (when a person's heart is right, he can go to bed on a pile of guns fourteen feet deep and never have a single thought about using a gun to shoot somebody). We don't have a drug problem, and we don't have a gun problem. We don't even have a legislative problem. We have a devil problem, and on top of that, we have a prayerlessness problem.

The second person who introduced me to the power of a mother's prayer was Mimi, my grandmother. She used to watch me so my mother could work her second job (both parents held down two jobs to make ends meet in those days). Mimi used to make me genuine peanut-butter-and-jelly sandwiches in those days. You can make that kind of sandwich only by mixing together the peanut butter and jelly in a bowl before piling about two inches of it on some homemade white bread that is so fresh that it sticks together.

I remember the time I climbed the steps in Mimi's house and looked around the corner into her bedroom. There was my grandmother, praying to God for her prodigal son, Willie. Mimi's husband had passed away, and she had only one place to go with her problems. I can still hear her desperate prayer: "God, wherever he is, save my Willie! The circle won't be broken. I'm trusting in You, Lord."[2] I don't know where Willie was that day, but he was probably in jail on a charge of public intoxication. That is where he spent a lot of his time in those days, but no matter where Willie was, Mimi was praying for him.

MIMI REFUSED TO LET GO

He used to come into Mimi's house with blood running down his face at times (presumably from bar fights), and I watched Mimi patch him up and then go into the other room with tears dripping off her cheeks. No matter how bad things looked, Mimi refused to let go. If somebody voiced a doubt about Willie's ultimate destination, Mimi replied, "Don't try to tell me my Willie will never get saved. The circle won't be broken! By and by, Lord, by and by, the circle won't be broken. He is faithful!"

She used to sing and pray over the kitchen sink while she washed dishes in her little white house. I can still see the tears running down her cheeks and falling into the soapy dishwater on a Wednesday night as she sang "Will the Circle Be Unbroken?" While she stood there with tightly wound pin curlers held in place with bobby pins, she sang the words, "There's a better home waiting in the sky, Lord, in the sky." On Wednesdays Mimi always moved a little quicker to be ready for church. She had some serious praying to do, so she wanted to get to God's house early. Her heart's cry in all of those years was, "God, save Willie."

A BONY ALCOHOLIC FINGER WENT UP IN THE AIR

Mimi went to heaven and never saw Willie come to Jesus, but I was there on the Sunday morning a bony alcoholic finger went up in the air after Willie said, "Enough is enough." More than a decade has passed since that day, and Uncle Willie is still sitting in the second row of World Harvest Church every Sunday morning. His transformed life is God's faithful answer to the travailing prayer of a mother who would not give up.

My praying grandmother taught her daughter how to pray. That daughter became my mother, and she taught *me* how to pray. My prayer is that every mature woman in the church of Jesus Christ will step up and take her rightful place as a spiritual mother, mentor, and instructor to the younger wives and mothers in the church.

I am convinced that we are losing a generation because we've failed to transfer into our children the anointing and spiritual treasures we received from a former generation. We need to repair a breach in the generational wall so we can impart the strength of God into the new generation.

As a pastor and father, I'm unwilling to entertain the young people under my influence. I'm looking for a generation of young remnant revolutionaries whose hands are trained for war. If I walk into a service or a youth function and tell them as their pastor, "It is time to watch and pray," I want to see young men and women drop down to their knees and get ahold of God to change a situation and their nation.

Mothers and grandmothers have played a key role in this area since the beginning of time, but too many mothers of the church are acting like spoiled spiritual teenagers. They demand that their pastoral staff counsel and pray unceasingly with them when they should be coming to services an hour early to teach the younger people how to pray, "God, give us souls lest we die!" *We need to hear mothers pray again.*

"COULD YOU COME? SHE IS DYING"

A young person who attended our church for some time was doing very well until her parents became offended for some reason. They pulled their daughter out of the church at the tender age of twelve or thirteen, and we didn't see them or hear anything from them for two years. Then I received a phone call: "Could you come? She is dying." It was that precious young lady. Parents, be careful not to leave a church for any reason other than a direct word from God. Never leave because you are offended; offense is something that can be dealt with. The consequences of disobedience can be another matter.

When I drove up the driveway of that home, those parents had the porch light on and the front door wide open. When they had left, they couldn't stand the sight of me; but on that day they couldn't wait for me to get there because their daughter was dying.

Those who are experienced in hospital visitation ministry often say they can smell death when they visit terminally ill persons in the final stages of their diseases. Well, I could smell death all over that house. When the parents opened the door to their daughter's room, I saw her lying on the bed and heard an indescribable death rattle coming from her throat as she struggled to gasp for a breath. Her body was emaciated, and her eyes were sunk back into her head. IVs and tubes were everywhere.

I wondered where the new pastor was, and then I saw him at the foot of the girl's bed. He and his wife had candles burning in the room, and they were kneeling in a formal prayer stance at the foot of the bed. The pastor's wife turned around to look at me and quickly turned back to tell her husband to make room for me. I asked one of the parents standing by the door, "What are they doing?" The answer was, "Oh, they're praying."

A righteous indignation came over me, and I ran into the room, slammed the door shut behind me, hurdled over the pastor and his wife, and climbed up in the middle of the bed. I pulled that dying girl into a sitting position and started praying with my eyes open, carrying a spiritual shield in one hand and the sword of the Lord in the other.

SHE NEEDED TRAVAILING PRAYER

I heard something slam behind me and found out the pastor and his wife had run from the room. They didn't stop running until they were in the car and squealing out of the driveway! None of that mattered to me at the time because there was a life in the balance. I looked into that girl's sunken eyes and said, "You spirit of death, I rebuke you in the name of Jesus Christ. Come out! Come out of her! Come out of her!" I didn't pray any religious prayers for that girl. She needed travailing prayer, and she got it. God graciously delivered her from the spirit of death that night.

Our children and lost family members don't need pampering;

they need our travailing and prevailing prayer. They don't need religion; they need to see the glory of God coming all over us. Do you want to change and melt the heart of that rebellious seventeen-year-old daughter of yours? Stand at your sink and wash the dishes after you've taken time to feed her. Let the tears drip off your cheeks into the dishwater, and let her hear you call her name before God.

"God, I know she's going out tonight. I know that what she is going to do isn't right, but I pray, Lord, that Your Holy Spirit will go with her. I pray, God, that You will give her an opportunity. Don't let her die in her sin and spend eternity hearing the howls and cackles from the bowels of a devil's hell."

GOD WANTS SOME GOOD WOMEN TO TRAVAIL AND PREVAIL IN PRAYER

God still answers prayer, but we need a few good women to answer the call to travailing, prevailing prayer. I remember the story an evangelist friend told me about an elderly woman at one of his evangelistic meetings. A particular church asked him to speak during a series of meetings, and he described the situation: "On the first night the hosts met me at the back door and said, 'Now this is your place in line.'" They had a large processional with beautiful organ music. He added, "It was like being waltzed in." The procession headed toward the platform, and just as my friend was about to round the corner of the front pew, he suddenly felt something grab him by the arm.

He said, "I looked around and discovered what it was. A little elderly woman with silvery hair and gold spectacles jerked the cane around my arm and said, 'Come here, Sonny.' She motioned for me with one frail finger, and when I bent down, she said, 'Are you praying, Sonny?' 'Well, yes, ma'am, I believe I am. I'm the evangelist for the service today.'"

My friend walked to the platform and sat down, but he told me he never really preached that night. "I could have preached in hell easier than I could preach in that place," he said. "There was such a stranglehold on that place, you could barely get your breath, but I tried to preach and give an altar call anyway. On the way out of the building, here came that cane again. 'Granny' pulled me down and said, 'Sonny, either you don't know how to pray, or you're not praying. Now you meet me here at three o'clock tomorrow afternoon.'"

YOU AIN'T MUCH, BUT YOU'LL HAVE TO DO

The evangelist walked into that building at three the next afternoon and discovered that eight silver-haired women were waiting for him. That little granny said, "We've been praying that God would send us an evangelist. You ain't much, but you'll have to do. We've been praying for revival to break out in this church, and we have also been praying for God to get ahold of this place and shake it like a rat terrier shakes a mouse. Now sit down there, Sonny; we're about to pray."

My evangelist friend said the next thing he knew, there were white hankies everywhere and the sweat was flying. Some of them were doing some kind of dance, and the rest of them were walking around laying their hands on the walls. They were screaming at principalities and powers, and they told the devil, "We *used* to shout in this church, and we're *gonna shout again!* We *used* to see sinners saved in this church, and we're *gonna see them saved again!* Devil, we bind you and cast you out in the name of the Lord Jehovah, His Son Jesus Christ, and by the power of the Holy Spirit!"

He said they had prayed for about an hour when all of a sudden, somebody said, "Gertrude, get the bag." One of the women, presumably Gertrude, pulled a large bag out from underneath the front pew and produced a giant, economy-sized bottle of cooking oil. Then they told the evangelist, "God told us to anoint this place with oil," and they started pouring oil into their hands.

Those aged prayer warriors didn't need to call on the church board, the deacons, or the Sunday school teachers to do their praying for them. They were part of a rugged remnant in that local church that remembered when the glory of God used to fill that house of prayer. They were tired of seeing the devil steal away their anointing, so they set themselves in battle array to watch and pray. They were ready to declare to the adversary in no uncertain terms: "We have been given power over all demons, and we possess power to cure diseases. We have been given power to tread on serpents and scorpions and over *all* the power of the enemy, and nothing shall by any means harm us." (See Luke 9:1–2; 10:19.)

O GOD, *MAKE IT HOT* IN THIS PLACE

My evangelist friend continued with his story: "I was still sitting there in that chair when the grannies pulled out that giant bottle of oil. Have you ever noticed how grannies have a special swing with the bottom of their arms when they are flinging flour or seed? These ladies were flinging that oil with that special swing, and it was sending anointin' oil all over that sanctuary. First they went for the pews with globs and handfuls of oil." He said, "Those grannies prayed, 'O God, *make it hot* in this place. *Make it hot!*'"

Those women knew they didn't have to be "religious" to catch God's ear. They didn't bother to throw in all of the thees, thous, and therefores favored by religious people. They knew that all they had to do was get an anointing.

My friend said that once the women felt that the pews were soaked well enough in the anointing (and the cooking oil), they started anointing the choir seats while praying, "*God, make it hot! Make it hot!*" Then they loaded up with oil again and anointed the organ, praying, "O God, *make it hot! Make it hot!*" Nothing seemed to escape their attention. They anointed every door, doorknob, seat, piano, piano bench, candelabra, speaker cabinet, and wall with that oil.

"I was still sitting there in that chair," he said, "when all of a sudden they looked at me in unison. The granny who started it all got a little curl in her wrinkled face at the corners of her mouth and a little smile broke out." He said she had prayed so hard that all of the bobby pins had fallen out of her hair.

SHE LOOKED LIKE SOME KIND OF COMBAT COMMANDO

"That silver hair was plastered down across her face in streaks of sweat, and she looked like some kind of combat commando," he said. "If I didn't know better, I would have thought she had on army boots. Then all of a sudden she started swinging that cane and announced, 'Let's get him, girls!'

"They converged on me," he explained. "They took that bottle of cooking oil and dumped it over my head. Then they rubbed it in for good measure. That wasn't a pentecostal church, but those grannies started to speak in other tongues as in the book of Acts. The next thing I knew, two or three of them had fallen out in the power and were rolling around on the floor groaning!" He told me, "Those women grabbed my hands and rubbed oil all over them. All I could do was sit there and weep in the presence of God."

It doesn't take many to turn the tide for righteousness, just a determined handful of people who are willing to pay the price for freedom. It takes some people who know how to get ahold of God. All it took in that church was a cane-swinging granny who declared, "I'm not going to let the devil keep his stranglehold on what God gave me."

My evangelist friend said he was still crying in his seat when the grannies packed up and left the building. They went through the same process every day until Sunday morning came around.

Once again the hosts met my friend at the back door and lined up in their religious procession. The line filed into the building as before, and when the evangelist started around the corner of the first row, Granny hooked him with that cane again. "Sonny," she said, "Holy Spirit told us today is the day. *It's gonna get hot in here today,* yes, sir."

"I HAVE NO EARTHLY IDEA WHAT I SAID"

My friend said, "As soon as I stepped behind that pulpit, something happened. I have no earthly idea what I said, but when I began to preach, I felt as if I were standing outside my body watching everything that was going on. I was saying things that I didn't know and had no way of learning."

Unknown to my friend, a very wealthy man in the congregation had held that church in absolute bondage under his ironclad fist. He was sleeping with another man's wife in the church and found solace and comfort by getting his conscience soothed in that church. Week after week, he used his wealth to control the church finances and hold the church under the bondage of his sinful lifestyle.

My friend told me, "Before I knew it, I found myself off the platform and well back from the front among the members of the congregation. With each new point, I moved along a particular pew toward the center of the row. Then I reached a point of quoting the Bible passage where Nathan the prophet confronted King David and said something like, 'What would you do if a man had done this and that?' The king responded, 'I'd have him put to death!'"

He didn't realize that as he reached that point in his message, he was standing right in front of that man. He said, "I pointed my finger at the man's chest, and under the anointing of the Holy Spirit, I quoted the final verse in the biblical confrontation of David when Nathan said, *'Thou art the man.'*

"The moment I said that, people gasped in shock throughout the building. The man I was pointing at looked as if he were going to tear my head off my shoulders, but when he stood up, something hit him in the stomach and threw him back about four pews! He got up and began to confess, 'I've held this church in bondage, and I haven't been right with God.'"

ARE THERE ANY GRANNIES IN THE HOUSE?

My friend said, "Before we knew it, seven hours had passed! People were lying all around the building where they had been slain in the Spirit and others were trying to stagger to their cars. People started throwing money on the pulpit, and a revival broke out that lasted for three months."

God is wondering, "Are there any grannies in My house today?" He declared through the prophet Jeremiah, "Call unto me, and I will answer thee, and show thee great and mighty things, which thou knowest not" (Jer. 33:3). Jesus said in the gospel of Mark:

> Have faith in God. For verily I say unto you, that whosoever shall say unto this mountain, Be thou removed, and be thou cast into the sea; and shall not doubt in his heart, but shall believe that those things which he saith shall come to pass; he shall have whatsoever he saith. Therefore I say unto you, what things soever ye desire, when ye pray, believe that ye receive them, and ye shall have them. (Mark 11:22–24)

We need to hear mothers pray again. We need an army of mothers and grandmothers who know how to change the world from their knees and pull souls out of the flames with their hot tears and travailing prayer. Nothing on earth or below the earth can escape the power of a praying mother who knows how to touch the heart of God in prayer. Even nature knows and fears the wrath of an angry mother protecting her young. It is time for the church to loose the power of her mothers' wrath into the streets of our disintegrating cities and threatening school halls.

The most feared demons of hell tremble when they hear those strident mothers' voices rising in righteous anger and holy wrath. They flee when they see Holy Spirit–filled white-haired grandmothers pray until their hairpins fall out and when they pull out their giant, economy-sized bottles of anointing oil and start slinging the anointing of God over every evil work they've done. Yes, it is time to hear our mothers pray again.

CHAPTER 12

RAISE UP EZEKIEL'S
BATTLE STANDARD
OF PRAYER

By the time we crossed the millennium line, our society had elevated physical passions and appetites to the level of gods. Along the way, the icons of American culture consigned restraint and self-control to religious nuts and moral extremists who were always trying to rain on their pleasure parade.

Where there is no control or restraint, the brooding and preserving presence of the Holy Spirit over the lives of humanity is conspicuously absent. The Spirit's holy presence is the only thing that preserves mankind from immediate destruction. He is the manifestation of God's mercy and grace on the earthly plane. He helps the spiritually blind discern the basic differences between good and evil and helps lead the lost to Christ. We need His power as never before in this society where right has been wrong for so long that righteousness is seen as an abnormality. That is the very reason we find ourselves planted right in the middle of it all.

Isaiah's ancient prophecy concerning the repopulation and restoration of Israel also applies to God's purposes for the church in America in the new millennium: "Remember ye not the former things, neither consider the things of old. Behold, *I will do a new thing; now it shall spring forth;* shall ye not know it? I will even *make a way* in the wilderness, and *rivers in the desert*" (Isa. 43:18–19, italics mine).

While many Christians are begging God to deliver them from this lost world, God has a different plan. He wants to bring new life to the spiritual desert we call America. The sand dunes of faithless living and hopeless dying are trying to encroach on the areas still sustaining life in our nation. The family is under continual assault, and the unholy coalition of our culture, our courts, and a core of highly vocal anti-Christian critics from coast to coast seeks to decimate godly values at every turn.

WE PRAY WITH THE FORMULAS, FORMALITY, AND PASSIONLESS PROSE OF YESTERDAY

Meanwhile, many of America's churches sleep on in filthy blankets of hypocrisy, poorly disguised sin, and stifling religiosity. Most of the churches that still believe in and practice prayer tend to go at it with the formulas, formality, and passionless prose of yesterday. We need to understand that pickle-juice expressions and a funeral-home demeanor mean nothing to God.

He isn't impressed with what goes for prayer on the other side of the house either. Mindless emotional fits, outrageous displays of fleshly excitement, and prancing egos performing under the pretense of prayer amount to nothing more than a powerless mockery of the real thing.

If God's purposes were limited to the power contained in our poor efforts at prayer, He would be forced to restore life in the spiritual desert of Isaiah's prophecy by using a child's squirt gun instead of the immeasurable supernatural resources at His command. Thank God, He can always rely on Himself.

This generation of revolutionary remnant believers is destined for an experiential manifestation and revelation of the glory of God. He brought us to the kingdom for such a time as this. God created and positioned us in time and space to be the vessels through which He will perpetrate His will upon this planet.

The first hint of God's plan appears in the book of Genesis where it is written, "And God said, Let *us* make man *in our image, after our likeness:* and let them have dominion" (Gen. 1:26, italics mine). The Son of God confirmed and expanded on this plan when He told the disciples:

> I will pray the Father, and he shall give you another Comforter, that he may abide with you for ever; even the Spirit of truth; whom the world cannot receive, because it seeth him not, neither knoweth him: but ye know him; for *he dwelleth with you,* and *shall be in you* . . . At that day ye shall know that *I am in my Father, and ye in me, and I in you.* (John 14:16–17, 20, italics mine)

What does all of this have to do with Ezekiel or a prayer standard? God is doing a new thing in this generation, something that is unprecedented in its depth and scope. When God moves in the earth, He does it through people. Supernatural power is released on earth only when the people of God become perfectly aligned and in agreement with Him, and when they pray *His way* to release entire rivers of anointing into the vast desert of thirsty human souls.

The things we are doing under the name of prayer aren't getting the job done. That can mean one of two things: God is doing something wrong (that choice isn't a real consideration), or *we* are doing something wrong. The answer is obvious, and the cure has everything to do with God and virtually nothing to do with us. God knows we don't know how to pray in our own strength and wisdom. He knows how miserable we are apart from His second-by-second guidance and empowerment. We live—and pray—by His mercy and grace alone.

WE ARE AN ETERNAL RACE OF SPIRIT BEINGS FITTED WITH EARTH SUITS

The first thing we did wrong happened when Adam sinned in the Garden of Eden and snapped our spiritual umbilical cord to God our Father. We were originally created and designed to be the exact likeness and mirror image of the Creator. In other words, God created a supernatural and eternal race of spirit beings fitted with earth suits for life on this planet. He fixed our terminal sin problem through His Son's sacrifice on the cross and the Resurrection three days later.

Ever since then, He has been waiting for a people who will pay the price to return to their calling as mirror images and exact representations of His glory in form and content. I can almost hear the Father explain to the Son how it will happen: "They are going to be in agreement with every eternal word that I have ever spoken. The Holy Spirit I have sent to them will anoint and energize every word that goes into their spirits. I will cause them to become priests and kings, and I will transform and remake them into a new species of being that has never existed before."

Just as the Canaanites of old were not prepared for the new generation of Israelites who crossed the river Jordan under Joshua's leadership, I assure you by the Holy Spirit that our celestial enemies are not ready for what is about to come across the Jordan in *this generation*. Satan and his hordes have never faced adversaries like these. They have never had to stand up to a people like this!

JESUS' PROPHECY SEEMS IMPOSSIBLE
AND PRESUMPTUOUS

I mean no disrespect to the heroes of the faith who blazed the trail before us with blood, sweat, and tears and an unyielding faith in God. We are here today because they stood by faith and made great sacrifices yesterday. Yet Jesus prophesied what seems impossible and presumptuous to the finite mind today:

> Verily, verily, I say unto you, He that believeth on me, *the works that I do shall he do* also; and *greater works than these shall he do;* because I go unto my Father. And whatsoever ye shall ask in my name, that will I do, that the Father may be glorified in the Son. If ye shall ask any thing in my name, I will do it. (John 14:12–14, italics mine)

Where are those works? We haven't managed to match most of the works of Jesus, let alone do "greater works." How can we once again become images of God and exercise dominion while walking in total agreement with His will?

About twenty years ago, God spoke to me in the night and said, "There is coming a day when they will no longer serve Me by being obedient to a body of written laws out of a spirit of fear." We know this is clearly spelled out in the Bible, but the problem is that Christians don't live and act as if they serve God out of love instead of fear. Like so many other great Bible truths, this truth isn't activated until it becomes a revelation all over again to each generation.

DO YOU HAVE A "GOD REFLEX" IN YOUR
LIFE AND SPIRIT?

Intimate relationship defines the difference between a casual, weekend Christian and an on-fire, Bible-believing, praying and prevailing, gospel-preaching radical remnant Christian. When you fear Him, no sacrifice is good enough. When you love Him, no sacrifice is too great. Love for God creates a reflex action in your life and spirit.

When you go to your doctor for a checkup, he will always check your reflexes. A reflex is a response to a stimulus that bypasses the conscious level. Immediate, strong reflexes are good, and reflexes that are delayed or unresponsive are bad.

Top athletes understand the importance of reflex actions. Regardless of the sport, the top contenders practice and discipline themselves for the love of the game and for another very important reason: disciplined practice and exertion help them go past the sticking point of thought and into the instinctive and almost instantaneous realm of reflex.

A black-belt karate instructor will parry a blow instinctively without thinking about it, whether or not he is on the job. If he competes against another black belt in a tournament, he won't have time to think about the hundreds of punches, blocks, counterpunches, and combination moves he will have to execute in a matter of minutes. He relies on his highly honed reflexes to carry him through.

An experienced competitor running the high hurdles doesn't slow down before each hurdle to calculate how high he should kick his lead foot, or whether or not his trailing knee will knock over the hurdle. These are the concerns of a novice with untrained reflexes. A seasoned hurdler rushes toward the obstacles at full speed, trusting the mechanics of the race to his reflexes so he can concentrate on the finish line.

AN UNSEEN UMBILICAL CORD
FROM HEAVEN PULLS ME UP

I don't go to church because I have to. I go to church even when every cell of my body is begging me to stay in bed; when my muscles throb, my lungs hurt, and my back aches. I go even when my body says, "No, rest," and my mind starts to agree with it. I have planted so much of God's Word in my heart that it acts like an unseen umbilical cord from heaven that pulls me off the couch, puts my feet on the ground, and sets me on my way. That is the Holy Spirit reflex action at work.

For about six thousand years, God has searched for people in every generation who would get in agreement with Him and train their reflexes for victory. The Bible is the family history of the Remnant Family of God. The members of this family are as different from one another as night is from day, except for one point: *they all prayed.*

They were male and female, strong and weak. Some were kings, but most were everyday people who knew how to pray and take God at His Word. Most of them had only a basic education, if that, and all but a handful were limited to the scriptures available in the Old Testament. Regardless of their credentials, they all prayed.

Most of us pray, too, but we can't measure up to "average" heroes in the Old Testament. What is missing from this picture? The people God used in the Old Testament didn't have any trouble figuring out the difference between their strength and God's strength because the Holy Spirit hadn't been released to live inside them yet. Whatever miracles happened in and through their lives came about because the Spirit of God dropped down on them for a while and did something impossible before leaving them again. Such events tended to keep them on their knees in desperate prayer much of the time.

WE ARE STILL TRYING TO PRAY IN OUR OWN WAY

We have the Holy Spirit dwelling inside us, but we take Him so much for granted that we need to rediscover the Divine Wonder living next door. In other words, we are still trying to do things for God—*such as pray*—in our own way, with our own strength, according to our own ways of thinking. (We are all well acquainted with the sorry results of our efforts.)

When the house of Israel woke up one day and found themselves weak, in bondage, and the laughingstock of the Middle East neighborhood, God spoke to them through Ezekiel the prophet about their problem:

> I will sanctify my great name, which was profaned among the heathen, which ye have profaned in the midst of them; *and the heathen shall know that I am the* LORD, *saith the Lord* GOD, *when I shall be sanctified in you before their eyes* . . . A new heart also will I give you, and a *new spirit* will I put *within* you: and I will take away the *stony heart out of your flesh,* and I will give you an heart of flesh. And I will put *my spirit within you,* and *cause* you to walk in my statutes. (Ezek. 36:23, 26–27, italics mine)

GOD'S SOLUTION TO THEIR POLLUTION WAS A RADICAL TRANSPLANT

God wasn't very happy about the way His people had profaned His great name with their rebellion and sinful ways (and He isn't very pleased with the way the modern church has smeared the name of Christ either). God's solution to their pollution was a radical heart and spirit transplant. Again, their cure was based on God's grace and mercy, not on their merit or ability. The Doctor has prescribed a "possession" as the cure for our self-obsession. If we are wise, we will yield to His friendly takeover.

Ezekiel prophesied in advance what Jesus prophesied in the fullness of time: "He that believeth on me, as the scripture hath said, out of his belly shall flow rivers of living water" (John 7:38). We think we know this, but we don't know how to live it. This is the foundation for world-changing, mountain-moving, devil-stomping prayer. This is God's prescription for *possessed prayer*.

The secret of possessed prayer and empowered ministry is found in the power of the Holy Spirit. Jesus said "rivers of living water" would flow out of the "belly" in John 7:38. Water often symbolizes the Holy Spirit in the Scriptures. The Authorized Version says all of this would flow "out of his belly," but that is a poor translation. The word translated "belly" is better translated "womb" or "incubation chamber."

I've noticed that the belly, or the most inward part of our being, functions in the spirit much like the human digestive system. It is like a generator that processes energy in one form to release another kind of energy throughout the body.

Workers on a remote construction site need electricity or compressed air to run their saws and drills. They solve the problem with a generator. As long as they supply that generator with energy in the form of gasoline, it will continue to produce plenty of converted energy in the form of electricity or compressed air.

WHAT INCREASES FAITH, IGNITES FIRES, AND CONVERTS WORDS INTO POWER?

The Holy Spirit does something similar as He bubbles and flows in your innermost being. He increases your faith, ignites your fire, and converts the eternal energy of God's Word into mountain-moving power! This power from heaven transforms your prayers and taps the unlimited power of God Himself.

God's Word is the fuel of heaven that empowers the words of our lips in prayer, declaration, and petition. Again, our problem is that we don't know how to convert heaven's energy into a form that will move obstacles and build the kingdom on earth. Left to our own devices, we revert to our forms, formulas, and intellect-based techniques and procedures.

God's solution to the problem is the same one Ezekiel described in the Old Testament. He wants to put a new spirit inside us. He wants to transplant new hearts in place of our stony and complacent hearts. Theologically speaking, God's Spirit came inside us when we were saved. In reality, most of us let Him inside, but we didn't give Him the run of the place. God didn't say anything about renting. He came in to take possession.

The only things God wants occupying space in His new house are the things of heaven, specifically His Word. The psalmist declared, "Thy word is a lamp unto my feet, and a light unto my path. I have sworn, and I will perform it, that I will keep thy righteous judgments. I am afflicted very much: *quicken* [revive] me, O LORD, according unto thy word" (Ps. 119:105–7, italics mine).

POSSESS THE WORD AND *BE POSSESSED* BY THE SPIRIT

God gave us the fuel of His Word, but we need a spark to ignite the fire and bring the coals to white-hot heat. He declared through Isaiah, "Thus saith the LORD, the Holy One of Israel, and his Maker, Ask me of things to come concerning my sons, and concerning the work of my hands *command ye me*" (Isa. 45:11, italics mine).

God gave us His Word, and He expects us to use it as a weapon of warfare against evil and as a tool of healing to raise up the sick and weary. Yet all of this still leaves us with the problem of fire. The church has held the power of God's Word in its hands for two thousand years, but it saw fit to declare miracles "a thing of the past" only a few generations after the apostles passed from the scene. Possession of the Word doesn't automatically mean you have the anointing and power of the Word.

God wants to see His purposes come to pass in the earth, but He has to light a fire underneath us to make the things He planted in our hearts come boiling up out of our spirits and burst forth on our tongues by the Holy Spirit. Jesus expects you and me to speak to the mountains and pray in unwavering faith in His faithfulness according to His promise in Mark 11:22–24.

GOD GETS HIS WAY AND USES YOU TO DO IT

Too many Christians believe they can pray for anything they want and expect it to happen. Jesus had no intention of giving the keys to the candy store to a bunch of sugar addicts. *When you are possessed by the Holy Spirit and in agreement with God's Word, whatever you pray will come to pass.* Why? God the Holy Spirit is doing the praying through you; it is not you. It amounts to God's getting His way and using you to do it.

God already sent us His Word. He gave us approximately 1,066 pages of it in sixty-six books, from Genesis to Revelation. His Word is filled with inspired sentences pregnant with miracle-working ability.

He put us on this planet with a temporary earth suit (our body) and equipped us with His Word as the law, a new uniform of righteousness in Christ, spiritual weapons, and a shield of authority as a badge. Now He expects us to impose His kingdom upon the darkness in this place.

Where there is sickness, we are commissioned to heal it. Where there is infirmity, we are called to restore it. Where there is hopelessness, we must bring hope. Where there is sorrow, we are to bring joy. How do we do it? We raise Ezekiel's standard of prayer. We yield to a total heart transplant and begin to practice *possessed prayer.*

JEREMIAH AND THE REMNANT CHURCH
SHARE A COMMON MISSION

Jeremiah wasn't always a prophet. He probably planned to live out his life as other people did until God apprehended him with a divine mission similar to the call to the modern remnant church:

> Then the LORD put forth his hand, and touched my mouth. And the LORD said unto me, Behold, *I have put my words in thy mouth.* See, I have this day *set thee over the nations and over the kingdoms, to root out, and to pull down, and to destroy, and to throw down, to build, and to plant.* Moreover the word of the LORD came unto me, saying, Jeremiah, what seest thou? And I said, *I see a rod of an almond tree.* Then said the LORD unto me, Thou hast well seen: *for I will hasten my word to perform it.* (Jer. 1:9–12, italics mine)

What was the significance of the "rod of an almond tree"? Almond trees are the first trees to bloom and signal winter's end in the Middle East. In the everyday vernacular of people in Columbus, Ohio, it was a sure sign that spring was about to break through the frozen landscape of a land locked in winter's grip. The Lord also used a play on Hebrew words to make an even stronger impression of urgency on His new prophet to watch and pray because a big change was in the wind.[1]

When you find yourself in the winter of your human experience, when it's so cold that you wonder whether your teeth will ever stop chattering, don't be surprised if God gives you a sign that a holy spring is coming. He will give you a word of hope when everyone else thinks you're crazy. If you dare to take Him at His word, then He will make *you* the early blooming almond tree that makes the heathen wonder! Every time it happens, remember that God is rushing toward you to perform His word, just as warm spring winds are rushing toward Jerusalem when the almond trees of Israel first bloom.

GO BEYOND MERE THOUGHT
INTO THE REALM OF HEAVENLY REFLEXES

When the Spirit of God breathes on the Word of God stored in your heart, it becomes a living part of your being. It goes beyond mere thought processes into the realm of heavenly reflex action. When a doctor gives you a bad report about a symptom in your earth suit, your spirit man's reflexes respond at the speed of light with the prevailing truth of God's Word.

I'm not teaching you a precept I pulled out of a dusty book somewhere. This is the way I have to live every day of my life. When you get a bad report, when the doctor says something is in your breast that shouldn't be there, when your child is in danger and you are too far away to reach him in the natural, the Spirit dwelling in your belly will begin to boil with holy heat. In a spontaneous reflex action not born of mental reasoning, you will declare the truth of God; you will act on what *you can't help believing!*

Don't expect to live this way if you spend more time with "flesh-a-vision reruns" than with Matthew, Mark, Luke, and John. Ezekiel gave the people an "almond blossom" hint of what was coming when God said through him that God was going to put a spirit in them that could cause them or make them walk in His statutes. When the Holy Spirit *possesses* you, He will make your appetites, cravings, and habits change for the good. Once the Spirit of God possesses your life, you will love reading your Bible more than you love watching the NFL play-offs (I really *am* believing for a miracle)!

THE HOLY SPIRIT SAYS,
"LET ME FINISH THOSE SENTENCES . . ."

At this stage, the spontaneous action of the Holy Spirit will literally finish every negative sentence of doubt and unbelief the enemy tries to bring into your life. The enemy speaks through a circumstance, trial, or temptation, and God sends His word in response that is so automatic, you won't think about it.

If the enemy says, "Die," before he can get past the *d,* your spirit will rise up out of your belly and declare, "Live!" Before the doctor can finish the word *sick,* you will say, "Well!" If your friends want to say, "Panic," you will say, "Peace," before they can say their piece. If the professional mourners try to say, "Sorrow," you will interrupt them to declare, "Joy!"

Once the Holy Spirit moves in and takes over, He starts to work on your sloppy and unresponsive reflexes. The more fuel you load in the hopper of your heart, the more firepower you pack in your gun. One of the biggest changes He makes in our lives is the way we pray. Out go the dry formulas, forms, and empty repetitions that used to be the favorites of the heathen until the church took up the practice.

You will pray all the time, whether it is convenient or inconvenient. A holy impulse to pray will grip you at odd hours of the night or at the grocery store or the office. Don't be alarmed. It is "God which worketh in you both to will and to do of his good pleasure" (Phil. 2:13).

YOU MIGHT FIND YOURSELF STANDING ON THE
WATER INSTEAD OF IN THE BOAT

I have to warn you about one more thing: it is inevitable that at sometime or another, the Spirit will take you farther than you have ever gone. You might find yourself standing on the water instead of in the boat. You will be facing a Goliath instead of watching the spectacle from the safety of the sidelines. You will be the one birthing a miracle instead of observing its arrival.

"David, how can *you* fight Goliath?" His Holy Spirit answer still stands today: "Is there not a cause?" He was the baby in the family, a young fair-faced boy with a knack for shepherding sheep, but a divine force was pushing him toward a great destiny.

"Hannah, why are you praying like that? Don't you know it isn't right to show that kind of emotion in a religious place? It isn't proper; in fact, I wish you would stop."

Her response to her priest was, "I would if I could, and I wish I could stop; but I can't. There's something in me that's too big to stop and too important to block."

If you are determined to move from passionless prayer meetings to marathon sessions of possessed prayer in the Holy Spirit, then be prepared to give up your independence and self-reliance. God will never create a life for you that renders Him unnecessary. The deeper you go into the things of God, the deeper you will have to go into *Him*. God will do everything that He has promised for us, but "He will be inquired of" concerning those things or He will not do them.

Prayer according to Ezekiel's standard is God-energized, God-directed, God-orchestrated, and God-centered prayer. This kind of prayer isn't generally associated with prayer cards and egg timers for carefully timed and orchestrated prayer. I am talking about something birthed by the Spirit of God. It is that "blooming almond tree" signaling the end of the seemingly endless winter. But remember this: it is the *possessed prayer* that becomes answered prayer only if it spontaneously bubbles up from the Holy Spirit dwelling in your innermost being. It is *possessed prayer* only if God is the Author and your tongue is but the pen of a ready writer.

CHAPTER 13

MANY INSTRUCTORS
BUT FEW FATHERS

A nation without fathers is a nation at risk. Disorder and destruction are soon to come, despite the valiant efforts of mothers and their fatherless children. America is reaping the folly of its second and third generations of absentee fathers who have the physical ability to reproduce but lack the most basic qualities of true manhood and fatherhood.

Many would like to portray the problem as something unique to particular races or to some economic demographic segment, but the truth is that this problem shows up in every race, economic stratum, and cultural group in America. Absentee dads among the rich are better able to hide their indiscretions and avoidance of responsibility, but wrong is still wrong and sin is still sin whether it is dressed up in bib overalls, gang colors, or a Hart Schaffner & Marx suit.

I established earlier in this book that as the church goes, so goes the nation. The root cause behind the loss of fatherhood in the home can be traced directly to the church's failures in the pulpit and in pastoral ministry.

Fatherhood is perhaps the most visible component of the divine DNA of God's image that was imparted to Adam. The heavenly Father created him to exercise dominion over the earth as a benevolent earthly father and steward, not as an emotionally removed tyrant. Adam's instinctive imprint for proper behavior came from the example that God modeled in front of him. In the same way, a godly father is God's chosen vessel to imprint a young man's heart for godly fathering in the next generation.

The apostle Paul took his role as a spiritual father very seriously, and I'm convinced God wants us to do the same thing today. Paul told the Corinthian believers:

> I write not these things to shame you, but as my beloved sons I warn you. For *though ye have ten thousand instructors in Christ, yet have ye not many fathers:* for in Christ Jesus I have begotten you through the gospel. Wherefore I beseech you, *be ye followers of me.* (1 Cor. 4:14–16, italics mine)

WE USE THE BLIND GUIDE DISCIPLESHIP PROGRAM

Evidently the church and society in general take their parenting and leadership training philosophy from a page in Matthew's gospel that records Jesus' description of the Pharisees' "blind guide" system (Matt. 23:16). Where there are no fathers, mothers are forced to do what they were never meant to do: train their sons to be men and fathers.

When the church has no spiritual fathers, those who have never led must train potential leaders. In some cases, young people who receive a call to the ministry must rely on the uncertain guidance of those who have never received and properly fulfilled a divine call to the ministry. Much of the time, they have no one to turn to. We have many instructors but few fathers.

I am convinced that there are very few active fathers in the church today, and there is a great need for their guidance in the church. A man in my church told me, "I'm just trying to find the will of the

Lord. I believe the will of the Lord for me is that I am supposed to be in ministry." He didn't realize that I knew what he was doing two days earlier when he sneaked around a corner to hide from me so he could smoke a cigarette. This man's back pocket is full of chewing tobacco, but he was ready to pastor a church.

I did what I am supposed to do as a spiritual father in God's house. I told him he didn't have any business going into the ministry as long as his habits controlled him rather than the other way around. In essence, I told him, "No, you know what you need to do. Sit down and hush. Put your feet under the table, and eat the Word until you grow."

THE HARVEST DISRUPTS OUR
LEISURE-TIME ACTIVITIES

This generation is teetering on the brink of something monumental and unprecedented in human history, but not everyone is interested or happy about it. The harvest disrupts the happy leisure-time priorities we've learned to love more than the work of God. Remember, Jesus said, "Behold, I say unto you, Lift up your eyes, and look on the fields; for they are white already to harvest" (John 4:35). He also said, "The harvest truly is great, but the laborers are few: pray ye therefore the Lord of the harvest, that he would send forth laborers into his harvest" (Luke 10:2).

The harvest field is whiter than ever, and the Lord of the harvest needs a trained workforce more in this day than in any other. Spiritual fathers are the primary "drill sergeants" who prepare the troops for battle in God's army. Spiritual mothers and women in general play key roles in the process, but fathers in the faith bear the greatest responsibility to train leaders for the next generation.

A modern disciple of Christ with a wise spiritual father doesn't waste his time looking for the will of God. He knows what too many

Christians tend to forget: that we are the sheep of God's pasture. According to God's Word, that means we are *supposed* to know His voice (John 10:4).

My little girl doesn't run to me every morning and say, "Oh, Father, my father. What is thy will for me today?" She doesn't go through all of that because she knows what I'm going to say: "Number one, hush. Two: Eat the corn flakes. Three: Go to the sink, rinse out your bowl, and put it in the dishwasher (your mama's not a maid). Four: Go upstairs and put on your school uniform. Five: Get the book bag—the one containing the *completed* homework. Six: Come back downstairs and get in the car. It is time to go to school."

WHY DO WE EXPECT GOD TO PUT UP WITH SUCH NONSENSE?

Wouldn't it be ridiculous for me to go through such an exercise with my daughter every day? Why, then, do we expect God to put up with such nonsense day after day? "Lord, I'm going to go to Dominion Camp Meeting and find the will of God." No, don't bother to come to our camp meeting to find God's will. It isn't something you find; it is something you live in every moment of every day. The Bible states, "The steps of a good man are ordered by the LORD" (Ps. 37:23).

You are in the middle of the perfect circumference of the absolute will of God for your life at this moment unless you're in rebellion. God has you exactly where He wants you right now. For your part, He asks that you be aware of the times and seasons and act accordingly.

My little girl understands what I expect of her, but she can't stay in my will if she has no way to know what time it is. If someone resets her alarm clock or changes her calendar, she might come running down the stairs on Sunday morning wearing her bathing suit or play clothes expecting to go outside and play. The only way she can stay in my will is to know what time it is.

Is it possible that the body of Christ seems to show up at the wrong place, at the wrong time, wearing the wrong kind of clothes because it doesn't know what time it is? We don't know what time it is because we don't have any daddies watching over our alarm clocks and calendars.

I have a mandate from God to tell the body of Christ what time it is. I am not the only timekeeper by any means, but I have an obligation to discharge my responsibilities without hesitation or apology. Some of us have on our party clothes, and the Master is waiting for us to get out in the harvest field! A good number of His kids in the North American church are still begging for crumbs underneath the Lord's table, while most of the others need to be pulled away from their gluttonous feast at the dinner table. The hungry ones are the first ones into the field, but the overstuffed people need to be pulled, pushed, encouraged, corrected, and pressed through the door and into the world.

JESUS PERSONALLY TRAINED TWELVE INTIMATE IMITATORS

We applied mass-production, fast-food-loving, power-merchandising techniques to the training of leaders and ministers of the gospel, then we wonder why they know so little about God or the kingdom. Jesus *personally* and intensively trained a core of twelve disciples (intimate imitators) and at least seventy more with basic instruction using question-and-answer methods and real-life application for three years. His students turned the world upside down.

Our new and improved fast-food version of discipleship and leadership training packs fifteen to fifty untested strangers into sterile seminary classrooms to be rammed through Bible knowledge courses like sardines through a processing plant. Sometimes there isn't a spiritual father within miles of the place, and God's presence is equally scarce. There are a few notable exceptions among our

Bible colleges and seminaries, but they are just that: *exceptions to the norm.*

This generation doesn't need any more men dispensing packets of instruction like computers that display files from memory banks full of dry Bible information. We need some discerning fathers who recognize that the source of our problem is the human heart. The church needs fatherlike leaders who realize that the mission of the Great Commission is to take the life of God to the hungry hearts of humanity.

WE DON'T NEED PREACHERS WHO SPUTTER OUT THE DEAD LETTER OF THE LAW

"Database Christianity" presents facts without understanding. It issues information without impartation. Remember the adage: as the church goes, so goes the nation. The power and witness of the church hinge on the quality of leadership behind our pulpits and on the streets. For two generations our attempts to reach our nation failed to produce a move of God because our preachers sputtered out the dead letter of the law. They touched the head and missed the heart of the people because they refused to pour the oil and the wine into the brokenness of the human experience.

No one should enter the ministry until his heart has been broken by the mercy and grace of God. The most successful ministers in God's kingdom are those who have failed so miserably that they will never forget the real Source of power, healing, hope, and joy in this world. In the terminology of Matthew Henry, failure produces "ownership of our dependence" on God, and that dependence should grow with greater success. These are the things best taught by and "caught" from spiritual fathers.

When God called me into the ministry, I was one of His most reluctant recruits. I grew up in a Free Will Baptist church in the 1950s and 1960s. By 1975, I was a senior in high school and the captain of the high school basketball team. One afternoon before a game, I wolfed down a good steak and French fries with lots of grease (I had arteries begging to be clogged) and lay down on my bed for a nap. Suddenly I saw the back wall of my room completely disappear—and my eyes were wide open. God began to give me an open vision.[1]

I saw a huge crowd and a lot of people who were crying out to be healed. One woman had a very large, swollen leg, and she couldn't get to the man on the platform because of the crowd. I remember weeping and crying out, "God, heal her, but don't let anybody know that it was me who prayed for her." I remember praying for the woman and watching God heal her leg. Then everything vanished.

I was just seventeen or eighteen years old, and I wasn't thinking about the things of God; I was getting ready for a basketball game. I can tell you this much: I wasn't worth anything on the basketball court that night after that vision.

I WAS A BAPTIST BOY: WE WEREN'T SUPPOSED TO SEE VISIONS

Keep in mind that I was a Baptist boy. We weren't supposed to see walls disappear or open visions appear in our bedrooms. That is why I didn't tell anybody about it. I began to feel a deep hunger in my heart, and I thought, *I know that there is more to this thing than what I have had.* Not long afterward, I received the baptism of the Holy Spirit in a pentecostal church service. A little later, I went to a secluded spot in the woods and found my favorite log where I liked to pray. I dared to ask God for more, and His Spirit descended on me in a way I had never known before.

I got up from that place and continued to feel the power of that visitation for many days. Despite the powerful visitations I experienced, I didn't know what to do with myself after graduation. All I knew was that I did *not* want to preach. My family always taught me, "If you can do anything else other than preach and still make a living, then do it." My mom was a real estate broker and my dad was a custom builder, so all I knew to do was to get a real estate license. I received the license, but no matter how hard I tried, it just wouldn't work. I was trying to hold down two secular jobs, and I was just miserable.

One day I was driving with my mother in Columbus, Ohio, and things were even worse. I kept losing jobs and it seemed that I was in the hospital all the time. I was so sick that I had to keep pulling over to the side of the road, and finally my mother looked at me and asked, "You are losing every job that you get, you are sick all of the time, and you don't sleep. What on earth is the matter with you?"

THAT IS THE CRAZIEST THING THAT I EVER SAID

I turned around and virtually screamed, "Maybe I want to preach!" Then just as quickly I said, "No, I don't. I don't want to preach." That was the first time I'd ever thought of it. I had a deep love for preachers. As a kid growing up, I didn't care who the preacher was. It didn't matter whether he was the darling of the denomination or a newcomer from the sticks. Whoever he was, the moment I recognized God on him, I would wrap my arms and legs around him and hold on. I often begged my parents to take me to the preacher's house. Then again, I had also seen the price preachers paid to preach the gospel. I had watched kids in school torment preachers' kids, usually for no reason at all. In spite of all that, I started preaching shortly after the incident in the car.

The second sermon that I preached lasted a grand total of seven minutes (some people wish that I would get back to that). I think I preached everything that I knew three times. Then I turned around to the pastor and said, "Well, that is all that I have to say." His response was literally, "Good. Praise the Lord." I promise you those were his words!

GOD SAID: *IT CAN'T GET ANY WORSE*

Back at home, I asked the Lord, "God, what am I going to do? I've made a mess of things." The Lord literally spoke up inside me and said, *It can't get any worse. It can only get better.* I kept right on preaching, and I'm happy to say that the Lord has helped me improve a little bit since then (even if I do preach a little longer these days).

Within a year of the car incident, I enrolled myself in Bible college because I thought that was what you did if you were called to preach. I thank God for what I learned during the three and a half years I spent in Bible college. At the age of twenty, my uncle and I started World Harvest Church with seventeen people in a little shelter house in my parents' backyard (it has grown a little since then). I knew I had to depend on God for everything I did.

I am quick to point to the fathers God placed in my life along the way. My earthly father imparted an invaluable example of godly character and faithfulness to me. He is still a doer of the Word, but he has never been much of a talker. The Lord also sent along other godly men to train me, but my real education in the ministry began when God linked my heart to the late Dr. Lester Sumrall, the founder of LeSea Ministries. He became my father in the faith and an apostle of the kingdom who gave me invaluable counsel and instruction.

Once I saw God's presence in him, I naturally wrapped my arms and legs around the man of God and wouldn't let go. He took me in as a spiritual son for fifteen unforgettable years. Dr. Sumrall has two sons who carry on his pioneering work in Christian media and world outreach to this day, and they were incredibly patient with this young upstart who joined their family.

Outlining all of the things Dr. Sumrall shared with me would take me weeks or months. He visited me often, and we discussed every aspect of my pastoral ministry in Columbus and the dangers and strengths of international television ministry. His wisdom and fatherly counsel saved me from trouble more times than I can count. I pray that every minister of God receives a spiritual father like I had. It can make the difference between success and failure, fruitfulness and unfruitfulness, in the ministry.

The transition from sonship to fatherhood is one of the most difficult passages in a minister's life. A dramatic change in my ministry occurred the year Dr. Sumrall suddenly went to be with the Lord, and it marked my unwilling transition from being a son to becoming a father.

As soon as the ministry in Columbus began to attract attention for its phenomenal growth and its aggressive outreach ministries, pressure mounted as people urged me to sponsor pastors' conferences, church growth seminars, and a ministerial fellowship.

I AVOIDED ANYTHING THAT RESEMBLED FATHERING

To be honest with you, I avoided anything that remotely resembled spiritual fathering. I became angry when people tried to force me into those activities. After Dr. Sumrall died, I realized I got upset because people were trying to make me be a father when I wanted to be a son. I knew I was a son to Dr. Sumrall, and if he walked on this planet today, I would still be a son. The seasons were changing, and it was time for me to follow God's lead.

The Lord prepared me for the change in a supernatural way just before Dr. Sumrall's death. Dr. Sumrall visited me at World Harvest Church in the month of April, and we were sitting around a conference table eating lunch with a couple of pastors. One of the men said to me, "I think you should have a pastors' conference."

That statement had been posed to me (and rejected) a thousand times. The pastor who said it was a friend, but he had no more influence in my life than anyone else. This time, however, something came out of my spirit, and I said, "I am going to. And I'm going to do it the second week in September." Then I put down my fork and said, "That's the craziest thing I've ever heard."

None of us in that room knew it, but Dr. Sumrall would go to be with the Lord within a week's time. He was as healthy as a horse, and his death came with no warning whatsoever. After he was gone, something in my makeup underwent a fundamental and radical change. All of a sudden I started caring about preachers and their churches in a way I had never known before. Before that time, I was consumed with the specific tasks God laid on my heart, and I didn't want to be diverted from those tasks.

DR. SUMRALL IMPARTED A MEASURE OF HIS FATHERLIKE SPIRIT TO ME

I started calling pastors on the phone, and I wrote them letters and prayed for their needs every day. It marked a 180-degree change in my life that has taken on a life of its own. Now my ministry to pastors is just as important to me as any other aspect of the ministry. My spiritual father, Dr. Lester Sumrall, had imparted a measure of his fatherlike spirit to me. Now I can't help pouring out my love, compassion, support, and fatherly guidance to the spiritual sons God sends my way.

Onlookers often see the father-and-son relationship in the ministry in a wrong light. Some people complain that it is a form of control over others that is ungodly. Others dismiss it as just another young buck trying to win points with the top man. I see it as God's pattern for maximum leadership and impartation of knowledge, wisdom, and anointing.

For years my friends and peers in the ministry used to make fun of me for being so devoted to Dr. Sumrall. I am close to these friends to this day, but they used to say, "Well, there he goes again. Wherever you see Brother Sumrall, you see Parsley." This is my counsel to any minister of the gospel who will listen: when God puts you in relationship with a seasoned man or woman of God, make sure you honor God's gift for what it is. If you wonder why God clothed His gifts in flawed human vessels who still have to deal with tempers, body aches, financial problems, and hormonal imbalances, then talk to Him about it. Meanwhile, remember that God knows what He is doing and we generally do not. Honor God's gift as something holy and worthy of respect. Listen, watch, and learn everything you can in the time you have been given. The day will come when others will be sent to learn from you.

OUR OWN SUCCESS CAN BREED DISRESPECT
TOWARD OUR FATHERS

Sometimes we show disrespect toward our spiritual fathers when we achieve some ministerial success of our own. We begin to compare our outward accomplishments to theirs, and then we consider ourselves their equal in terms of success.

Preachers' egos have a tendency to stretch out of shape as it is, and it doesn't help when people treat us like royalty because they hope to gain something from their relationship with us. I went through a dark period when some of my peers were asked to preach in Dr. Sumrall's national conferences.

No matter who was preaching in those conferences, I considered it my duty to be there in the eighth row. Then I noticed that when things changed and I was the one invited to preach, very few, if any, of those peers were in the meeting. I loved my friends (and they remain good friends to this day), but at that time they didn't understand that I didn't go to meetings just because I wanted an opportunity to preach. I would have been in my seat on the eighth row even if I had never preached at those conferences. (Honestly it is harder to preach in those meetings than anywhere else in the world. Preachers make for a tough audience.)

PREACHERS WHO HUNT RECOGNITION AND EXPOSURE ARE SHOOTING STARS

I am convinced that there will be a great renaissance of father-and-son relationships, respect, and honor in the ranks of the ministry in the days to come. Dr. Sumrall used to call the young preachers who were always hunting for recognition and exposure shooting stars. One year you see them on the covers of the leading Christian magazines and their names are household names in church circles. Then five years later, you never hear of them again.

All across the country, called and anointed ministers are seeking a foundation in their lives. Perhaps they didn't feel a need for it before, but God has a way of showing us how much we need friends, brothers (and sisters), and fathers in the faith. It all goes back to the reverent fear of our sovereign God, and the respect we show for His presence in one another.

My respect for my spiritual father didn't change because my church grew to a size that was fifteen times larger than his, or because my television ministry was larger than his. Dr. Sumrall was an apostle of the faith, and God assigned him to be my spiritual father. If I lived to the age of Methuselah, had the wisdom of Solomon and the tenacity of Paul, I would still respect and honor Dr. Sumrall for what he was: my spiritual father.

I never called him "Doc," and I never called him "Les," "Lester," or "Hey, Sumrall." Several years after his death, I still refer to the man who brought me into ministerial maturity as Dr. Lester Sumrall. He shared with me that he felt the same way about his spiritual father,

Howard Carter. He said, "Dr. Carter was twice my age, but he had it [the anointing], and I wanted it, and that made us good friends." I have to say that Dr. Sumrall was twice my age too. He "had it" and "I wanted it"; and we were a good match too. We spent fifteen years together as spiritual father and son, and I miss him every day.

Spiritual fathers, just like natural fathers, cannot afford to subscribe to the modern theory that they "need to be their kids' best friends." It is great to be friends, but the establishment must be in authority, and friendship must remain a by-product. If I am your friend, then we are on equal footing, and I strip you of the stability that is gained by structure. Every human being longs for boundaries. We thrive in them. When the boundaries are removed—where there is no vision—the people run wild. Friendship doesn't require you to set boundaries in the lives of others. Fatherhood does.

A river without banks is not a river; it is a swamp. The church has almost reached a standstill today. The flow of the life of God has been slowed to a trickle as the people of God lay before Him in inactivity, apathy, and lack of direction. This is the season for the fathers of the church to arise and restore the boundaries, direction, and the flow of divine life to God's house. Many churches don't like to use the term *apostle,* but since God saw fit to use it in the Bible, I'll use it too.

Where are the fathers? Lord, raise up Your apostles today, and command them to take their place before the people. There are sons who are waiting for a God-ordained adoption in the Spirit.

CHAPTER 14

BREAKTHROUGH
DEMANDS THE
SPIRIT OF A BREAKER

Millions of blood-bought people across this nation are strategically positioned on the edge of the unknown. They are on the verge of a curious mystery, and they feel a strange urge. They are poised on the brink of the unthinkable, and they wonder what happens next. I am one of more than a few sent on a God-mission to the people on the brink.

The Lord told me what He wants me to do when I reach them. It happens every time I step behind a pulpit in a new city or auditorium. It happens every time I step in front of a television camera or Bible school class. The Lord never sends me to catch them and save them from a fall. Neither does He send me to urge them away from the edge of the brink. The purpose of my mission is shocking to most; but there are a few, a revolutionary remnant crew, who understand the divine purpose behind it all.

God sends people like me to people on the brink for one reason. He said, "It is I who put them on the edge and positioned them on the brink. Now I expect you to push them over the edge, plunge them into the brink, press them to stretch beyond all they could hope or think."

If I hear the word of the Lord accurately—and I know that I do—then by the time you complete this chapter, you may well find yourself in a place you didn't know existed and doing things you didn't think were possible. In fact, there is a chance that God's hand is on you to give birth to a miracle (though you didn't even know that you were pregnant)!

Don't fall into the religious mode and say, "Pastor Parsley is talking about giving me more of what I've already had." I am not talking about the anointing we define with a "dippity-doo, little dab will do you blessing" or a "courtesy drop" to the floor after someone lays hands on us. This is something altogether different. This has the mark of awe on it; it has the mark of the immeasurable and the irresistible about it. Something about it defies definitions and boundaries. There is more of God than man in this thing.

THIS ANOINTING IS RESERVED FOR THOSE WHO HAVE PLUNGED OVER THE BRINK

Some Christians spend so much time in the anointing line so people can anoint them with oil on their foreheads that they look like greased pigs at a county fair. The anointing I'm talking about is too big and powerful for casual handling. It is reserved for a people who have plunged headlong over the brink of their limitations and fears to pursue God's purposes. There is a holy weight to this anointing that demands God's help just to bear up under it. God will have to strengthen your legs, support your back, and brace your shoulders to help you stand up under the weight of this anointing.

God said something that might help you understand where we are going as a revolutionary remnant on the brink of destiny: "I will go before thee, and make the crooked places straight: I will break in pieces the gates of brass, and cut in sunder the bars of iron: and I will give thee the treasures of darkness, and hidden riches of secret places" (Isa. 45:2–3).

The Lord is ready to bring a breakthrough anointing to His remnant people. A *breakthrough* is "a sudden burst of the advanced knowledge or revelation of God that will propel you through every line of Satan's defense."

You have hoped long enough. You have believed, prayed, fasted, clapped, and shouted long enough. In the words of some of my congregation members, "You have preached long enough!" You have confessed it, but you haven't possessed it. It is time for a breakthrough.

PETER HAD A REVELATION AND SAID THE UNTHINKABLE

Peter had a breakthrough the day Jesus asked His disciples, "Whom do men say that I the Son of man am?" (Matt. 16:13). The disciples operating in common knowledge said He might be John the Baptist, Elijah, Jeremiah, or one of the other prophets who were raised from the dead. But Peter didn't name any of those people. When Jesus made it more personal and asked the disciples who *they* thought He was, Peter stepped into the realm of divine revelation and said the unthinkable:

> Simon Peter answered and said, *Thou art the Christ, the Son of the living God.* And Jesus answered and said unto him, Blessed art thou, Simon Barjona: for *flesh and blood hath not revealed it unto thee, but my Father which is in heaven.* And I say also unto thee, That thou art Peter, and upon this rock I will build my church; and the gates of hell shall not prevail against it. And I will give unto thee the keys of the kingdom of heaven: and whatsoever thou shalt bind on earth shall be bound in heaven: and whatsoever thou shalt loose on earth shall be loosed in heaven. (Matt. 16:16–19, italics mine)

This is the season of Holy Spirit possession. The Holy Spirit can go where you can't go. He can hear what you can't hear and reveal it to you right when you need it. When He reveals such a thing to you, it builds your faith so you can do what you thought you could never do.

BREAKTHROUGHS COME ONLY WHEN YOU NEED BREAKTHROUGHS

Remember that breakthroughs never happen in good times or stress-free periods of history. Breakthroughs come only when you face some things you need to *break through*. Our God has a very interesting trait that plays a big part in the breakthrough anointing I'm talking about. This interesting trait of the Divinity shows up in the book of Exodus:

> The LORD spake unto Moses, saying, Speak unto the children of Israel, that they turn and encamp before Pihahiroth, between Migdol and the sea, over against Baalzephon: before it shall ye encamp by the sea. For Pharaoh will say of the children of Israel, They are entangled [perplexed] in the land, the wilderness hath shut them in. *And I will harden Pharaoh's heart, that he shall follow after them; and I will be honored* upon Pharaoh, and upon all his host; that the Egyptians may know that I am the LORD. (Ex. 14:1–4, italics mine)

I'm sure that God didn't want to take the Israelites to the brink of a heart attack when He arranged for them to be cornered between Pharaoh's chariots, the mountains, and the sea. However, it isn't His nature to hide and scamper away from those who defy Him. It may not be politically correct, but God is confrontational. Let me put it another way: the God we serve likes to pick a fight with His foolish enemies (that is the only kind He has).

THE ISRAELITES WHO COULDN'T SWIM
WERE ASKING, "WHY ME?"

God clearly explained in His Word that He personally arranged for Pharaoh to know where the Israelites were, and He made Pharaoh so mad that he forgot all about the suffering his hard head had already brought to his household and his nation. I imagine that at least one or two of the Israelites—especially the ones who couldn't swim—were asking themselves, "Why would God let this happen to me?" God wasn't going to let anything happen to them except for a miracle. He orchestrated the whole thing for His glory. We are in the same situation now.

We don't need to worry about the brink, the verge, the edge, or the abyss. God is on our side. We generally see defeat in our situations, but He always sees victory. The King James Bible says that when the Israelites reached the Red Sea, the Lord sent a strong east wind and "the waters were divided" (Ex. 14:21).

The original Hebrew word, *baqa'*, literally means "to rend, break, rip or open: to make a breach, break forth."[1] That body of water blocked their way to freedom and God's land of promise, so the Lord *broke it up*. It was a good thing too. The Israelites needed a breakthrough miracle on their first day out of bondage. Their armed and angry enemies were right behind them, and they had no place to run.

The Israelites walked into freedom and victory over Pharaoh that day without a single weapon drawn or arrow put in flight. God fought the battle for them, and they were on their way to the land of promise. They made the journey to the river Jordan and the boundary or brink of promise and turned back in doubt and unbelief. It took forty years of wandering and a new generation before God could demonstrate His delivering power to the Israelites once more.

WE STEPPED OUT OF THE SECOND DAY
AND INTO THE THIRD DAY

The Bible says, "One day is with the Lord as a thousand years, and a thousand years as one day" (2 Peter 3:8). That means that when we stepped into this new millennium, we stepped out of the *second day* and into the *third day* of our new freedom in Christ! Do I need to remind you what happens on the third day in God's world? (That is when things that are dead come to life again.)

We are like the new generation of Israelites poised on the brink of destiny while the waters of the river Jordan flowed at flood stage in the time of harvest (Josh. 3:15). If you are like some believers, then you are just too happy to continue wandering in the wilderness like second-day Christians. You have no interest in claiming another pair of shoes that didn't wear out. That is yesterday's miracle and yesterday's message.

Don't stay in the wilderness of yesterday. Come with me, and follow the Lord to the river Jordan. Calm your fears, and come to the edge of the water. I know the water is running at flood stage because the harvest season is here. Hear Joshua say, "Come on and gather around this Jordan, for in three days' time, we are crossing over this river into our destiny."

THEY NEEDED GUIDANCE,
FOR THEY HAD NOT PASSED THIS WAY BEFORE

It came to pass after three days, that the officers went through the host; and they commanded the people, saying, When ye see the ark of the covenant of the LORD your God, and the priests the Levites bearing it, then ye shall remove from your place, and go after it. Yet there shall be a space between you and it, about two thousand cubits by measure: come not near unto it, that ye may know the way by which ye must go: for ye have not passed this way heretofore. (Josh. 3:2–4)

THE LEADERS HAD TO COME TO THE BRINK AND TAKE THEIR STAND BY FAITH

Thou shalt command the priests that bear the ark of the covenant, saying, When ye are come *to the brink of the water* of Jordan, *ye shall stand still* in Jordan. (Josh. 3:8, italics mine)

THE PRIESTS OF GOD BEAR HIS PRESENCE TO THE VERY BRINK OF THE HARVEST

As they that bare the ark were come unto Jordan, and the feet of the priests that bare the ark were dipped in the brim [brink] of the water, (for Jordan *overfloweth all his banks all the time of harvest*). (Josh. 3:15, italics mine)

LEADERS MUST STEP OVER THE BRINK AND STAND FIRM SO OTHERS CAN CROSS OVER

The priests that bare the ark of the covenant of the LORD stood firm on dry ground in the midst of Jordan, and all the Israelites passed over on dry ground, until all the people were passed clean over Jordan. (Josh. 3:17)

When the time came for Jesus to launch His earthly ministry in Jubilee, He came out of the wilderness and entered the synagogue in His hometown. Then He read the familiar passage in Isaiah 61 in a way that was unfamiliar to the people in that meeting. He said,

The Spirit of the Lord is upon me,

because he hath anointed me to preach the gospel to the poor;

he hath sent me to heal the brokenhearted,

to preach deliverance to the captives,

and recovering of sight to the blind,

to set at liberty them that are bruised,

to preach the acceptable year of the Lord. (Luke 4:18–19; Isa. 61:1–2)

JESUS ANNOUNCED WHAT NO ONE HAD EVER DARED TO SAY BEFORE

According to the Bible, Jesus closed the book and gave it to the minister. Then He sat down and waited for everybody to settle down before announcing what no one had ever dared to say before: "This day is this scripture fulfilled in your ears" (Luke 4:21).

If you keep reading, you will notice that in a matter of minutes, that religious group of worshipers was doing its best to throw Jesus off the edge or brink of a hill, but Jesus passed "through the midst of them" (Luke 4:29–30).

The Bible records that Jesus came in "the fullness of the time" (Gal. 4:4). The "fullness of the time" can also be properly translated "in due season" or the "season of completion."[2] Every woman who hears me talk about "due season" or the "fullness of the time" instinctively understands its importance. When something reaches its due season and the fullness of time, that means it's time to finish this thing; it's time to deliver; it's time to break through and break out!

God set the world into motion, and when Adam sinned, He set His eternal plan of redemption into motion as well. I can hear the Almighty saying from His throne, "I've set My clock. When time gets full, you are about to pass through."

ISAAC WAS A DELIVERING CHILD
BORN OUT OF IMPOSSIBILITY

Have you wondered why you felt so pressured and squeezed over the last few years? Do you feel as if you live in perpetual darkness, and every time you try to push out, something pushes you back? As we noted earlier, Father God, the Ancient of Days, has gone into Mother Time and has conceived a child of His old age, the delivering child.

The book of Genesis tells us that Judah, one of Jacob's twelve sons, conceived a child with a woman named Tamar:[3]

> It came to pass in the time of her travail, that, behold, twins were in her womb. And it came to pass, when she travailed, that the one put out his hand: and the midwife took and bound upon his hand a scarlet thread, saying, This came out first. And it came to pass, as he drew back his hand, that, behold, his brother came out: and she said, *How hast thou broken forth? this breach be upon thee:* therefore his *name was called Pharez.* And afterward came out his brother, that had the scarlet thread upon his hand: and his name was called Zarah. (Gen. 38:27–30, italics mine)

THE CHURCH TRIES TO COME OUT "ARM FIRST"

I don't mean to give you an obstetrics lesson, but anytime a baby begins to emerge from the birth canal arm first, you have trouble. The church is always trying to come out "arm first" because we try to accomplish supernatural things through the arm of the flesh. The midwife was careful to put a scarlet thread around the protruding wrist because she thought it signaled the coming of Judah's first-born child. That title carried with it the birthright and the inheritance of everything Judah had. The midwife was upset when that arm—and her pretty scarlet thread—was jerked back into the womb.

There was another baby in that womb, and Baby Number Two said, "Excuse me, but I don't think I'm going to lie around in here while you take what rightly belongs to me. Get your arm back in here!" The Bible tells us that second baby came through the birth canal *head first*.

My wife, Joni, labored for thirty-six hours before the doctor bothered to show up. I kept asking where he was, and the nurses kept saying, "Oh, he'll be here." At the end of the thirty-sixth hour, a nurse rushed out of the room and the doctor dashed in! He had nurses pulling latex gloves on his hands while another tried to drape a surgical gown around him and fit his face with a mask.

When he knocked me out of the way, I said, "What's all of the rush about now? Thirty-six hours and you didn't bother to come around here until now." Do you know what he told me? He said, "That baby's head is crowning!"

Consider this passage in the book of Ephesians:

> According to the working of his mighty power, which he wrought in Christ, when he raised him from the dead, and set him at his own right hand in the heavenly places, far above all principality, and power, and might, and dominion, and every name that is named, not only in this world, but also in that which is to come: And hath put all things under his feet, a*nd gave him to be the head over all things to the church, which is his body.* (Eph. 1:19–23, italics mine)

WHERE THE HEAD GOES, THE BODY HAS TO FOLLOW

Micah the prophet declared to Israel, "*The breaker* is come up before them: they have broken up, and have passed through the gate, and are gone out by it: and their king shall pass before them, and the Lord on the head of them" (Mic. 2:13, italics mine).

Do you know what they named the baby who came out head first ahead of the one they thought would be the firstborn? The English transliteration of his Hebrew name is given variously as *Pharez* and *Perez*. It means "to break through, break down, break out" or simply "the breaker."[4]

God is going to have a people, and He is going to have His day when His revolutionary remnant people, full of His Spirit and resplendent in His shekinah glory, will walk across the face of the earth in absolute dominion and victory. Whether the enemies of God like it or not, we are the Breakthrough Church, and we have entered the fullness of time.

There are about to be a revolution and an overthrow of the gates of brass and bars of iron the enemy has erected in front of you. The King of glory has ordained you and me to be breakers on a mission from God. The gates of hell are coming down in the earth because the spirit of the breaker is upon us!

This holy spirit of supernatural power shows up throughout the Scriptures in times of special need and eternal urgency. Do you remember the man named Mahalaleel, the son of Seth, the son of Adam? Mahalaleel's name means "praise of God," but when it is broken down to its fullest meaning, it also means "to break through as by ramming with the head"![5]

BE A BONEHEAD FOR CHRIST

Mahalaleel symbolizes breakthrough praise, which rams every obstacle with the head of the authority of Christ. It breaks through every door of darkness, it breaks up every bar, and it breaks down every demonic gate of brass blocking our way! That is the spirit God placed within you.

Judah had a son named "the Breaker." The Breaker had a son through many generations named Joseph. Joseph had a son through more successive generations who was wrapped in swaddling clothes and lay in a manger.

John wrote of that Son: "In the beginning was the Word, and the Word was with God, and the Word was God" (John 1:1). He also wrote, "But as many as received him, to them gave he power to become the sons of God, even to them that believe on his name" (John 1:12).

God restored Adamic authority in the earth through the death, the burial, and the resurrection of His Son, Jesus Christ, and through the intervening agent of the Holy Spirit who possesses men and women in the earth. (Don't let anyone talk you out of something God gave His Son to provide for you.)

The name Perez also appears in Nehemiah 11 where God told the prophet to repopulate His holy city with "one in ten" of the people. He wanted the "tithe" or firstfruits of the people, not everybody. It was time to take over, and God was handpicking His pioneers and rebuilders of the breach.

A BREAKER PRODUCES AN ARMY OF VALIANT MEN

Everything went as planned until you read who represented the descendants of Judah. It started with a man named Athaiah. He just happened to be listed as the seventh in line from *Perez* through his son *Mahalaleel*! Was this an accident? Absolutely not.

All of the other families sent one in ten of their sons to help repair the breach and restore Jerusalem. Not Athaiah, the descendant of Perez, the Breaker:

> Of the children of Judah; Athaiah the son of Uzziah, the son
> of Zechariah, the son of Amariah, the son of Shephatiah, the son of

Mahalaleel, *of the children of Perez* . . . All the sons of Perez [the Breaker] that dwelt at Jerusalem were *four hundred threescore and eight valiant men.* (Neh. 11:4, 6, italics mine)

God told the people to bring one in ten, but the children of Mahalaleel (breakthrough praise), descended through Judah (celebrated), of the sons of the Breaker, brought 468 *valiant men.* It gets even more interesting than it already appears because the word *valiant* doesn't mean what we think it means. The original Hebrew word is *chayil,* and it means "a force, whether of men, means or other resources; an army, wealth, virtue, valor, strength."[6]

God is giving birth to a revolutionary remnant force of valiant men and women. He has given us the spirit of a breaker and made us valiant. We are a divinely equipped and empowered force to be reckoned with. By His Spirit, He has equipped us with everything necessary to break through, break down, or break up those things opposing us. We possess all things necessary for total victory: all the means, resources, wealth, virtue, valor, or strength that we need!

WE ARE GOD'S VALIANT BAND OF BREAKERS

God is about to bear down and give birth. He intends to perpetrate His will in the earth through a valiant band of breakers into whose hands He can place the substance necessary to overpower every force of the enemy.

Let me balance this powerful word with a sobering warning. This calling and anointing is not for the weak or the uncertain. It is given only to those who are willing to step over the line and into the brink of absolute commitment and sold-out obedience to God. The moment you do that, you become the sworn enemy of the adversary, and he will do everything in his power to knock you out, bring you down, or divert you from the path God intends for you.

I've realized that everyone who has accomplished great things in God's kingdom suffered a great attack, setback, or catastrophe in his life or in his family. I'm not talking about a curse or some twisted idea that God likes to hurt those He loves. I am warning you that God's enemy is also our enemy, and he especially despises the people who have power to damage his kingdom.

When my promised child, Austin Chandler, was only three and a half years old, my wife and I took him to the Cleveland Clinic to check out some serious abnormalities we noticed. The doctors handed him back to me after their examination and said, "Mr. Parsley, we have a psychiatrist available here. No, his services are not for your son. They are for you and your wife. When parents hear news like we have to share with you, they often fall to pieces."

DON'T EXPECT HIM TO CALL YOU DADDY

They told Joni and me that our son had the IQ of a genius, but then they added, "Don't ever expect him to call you Daddy. Don't expect your son to go to school or ride a bike. He won't play with other children in a normal way because he has a neurological disorder called autism, Reverend Parsley. There is no treatment and no cure for this disorder. We're sorry, but there's no hope."

There wasn't a Hammond B-3 organ nearby that day, and nobody was preaching in the parking lot of the Cleveland Clinic when I held my baby in my arms and walked that endless walk with tears dripping off my face and onto my child.

I began to sing,

> My hope is built on nothing less
> Than Jesus' blood and righteousness.
> I dare not trust the sweetest frame,

> But wholly lean on Jesus' name.
> On Christ, the solid Rock, I stand,
> All other ground is sinking sand.

I looked at my wife, Joni, and said, "Honey, you know the revelation that God has given us for this boy: he is the seed of promise, an answer to prayer and a perfect gift from God. You know what Cornelius did. You know what Hannah did. You know what Jephthah did too. God will require no less of us. I must see this thing broken; I must see my seed given back to me!"

God led me back to the third chapter of the book of Malachi, and I reread that familiar passage we tend to associate exclusively with the tithe and the financial principles of the kingdom:

> Bring ye all the tithes into the storehouse, that there may be meat in mine house, and prove me now herewith, saith the LORD of hosts, if I will not open you the windows of heaven, and pour you out a blessing, that there shall not be room enough to receive it. *And I will rebuke the devourer for your sakes,* and he shall not destroy the fruits of your ground; neither shall your vine cast her fruit before the time in the field, saith the LORD of hosts. (Mal. 3:10–11, italics mine)

DEVOURER MEANS "SEED EATER"

I believed God's Word. He wanted to pour out a blessing for us that would stagger us. At that point, I was even more interested in His promise to rebuke the devourer. God promised He would tell the devourer, "That's enough! Stop it. Don't come one step farther." I also remembered that Oral Roberts told me the word *devourer* means "seed eater."

When the ancient Israelites wanted to lay claim to some land,

God told them to dig a well and sow a seed. Then He would give it to them. In my spirit, I saw my beautiful, healthy son just on the other side of a field. God said, "When you sow the seed to claim this field, I, the Lord your God, will go out to the edge of where you have sown your seed and stand guard. When the enemy approaches the edge of your sown field, I will personally rebuke him!"

I told my wife, "Honey, I know what we have to do. This is the greatest need of our lives, so we have to sow the greatest seed we have ever sown in our lives. God spoke to me and said, 'I'm going to make it a resurrection seed. I will make it a *third day seed*.'"

How did Jesus buy our salvation? He became a *Seed* planted in a borrowed tomb. Praise God, the Seed has life in itself. Three days later that divine Seed *broke through*. I am talking about the miracle harvest of a resurrection seed.

God told me an amount of money to put in my hand and said, "When you put it on the altar, I will rebuke the seed eater for your sake." I told my wife what we were to sow, and in our combined bank accounts, we did not have a tithe for the total amount of money God told me to sow. I said, "I'll put my faith on the line, and I'll find it. He told me what to do, and I'll find it."

GOD WILL WALK TO THE EDGE OF YOUR SEED AND REBUKE THE SEED EATER

Ten days later I came back with a seed in my hand. It was a staggering amount to us, and ten days earlier we didn't even have a tithe on that amount. When I got back to World Harvest Church, I called God to record as He asked us to in His Word. I said, "You promised me that if I sowed this seed, You would rebuke the seed eater. By faith I sowed the seed, and I believe that You are going to walk out to the edge of this seed and rebuke the devourer. I believe that the breakthrough anointing on this seed is going to break through in the life of my son—in spite of the fact that the doctors said there was no treatment, no cure, and no hope."

At the time of this writing, my son is eight years old and in the second grade (like most eight-year-olds). He has never made a B because he makes straight A's. Now this means a lot to me because even though I have watched people walk out of wheelchairs on a regular basis in my ministry, my own child is supposed to be sitting in a room pounding his head on the side of a wall, drooling, and not speaking to anybody.

God overthrew the system and set my son free! My boy reads the reading lesson to the fifth-grade class at school. I am standing on the victory side of a resurrection seed! Now God has anointed me to tell you that the spirit of a breaker is upon you and all of your seed too!

Remember that God does nothing by accident or by chance. You are reading these words because the sovereign God ordained that it would be so. God moved you to the edge of your comfort zone and positioned you on the brink. He didn't link our lives together through these pages just so I could warn you about the dangers of living close to the edge. He didn't send me to protect you from the brink. My job is to push you over the edge and plunge you into the brink. It is time. God is pushing you into your destiny. He is prodding you over the edge.

Dare to let Him stretch you beyond all you could ever hope or think. If you need a breakthrough, then you need to receive the spirit of a breaker.

NOTES

CHAPTER 1

1. You may wonder why Enoch talked about the Second Coming and not the Rapture. Why would he talk about something that had already happened to him? Enoch would experience his own personal preview of the Rapture when God "took him" from this planet before judgment came to his generation. As far as the vision goes, he would already be with the Lord, just waiting for the rest of us to catch up.

CHAPTER 2

1. Frederick Douglass, cited in *The Great Quotations: A Unique Anthology of the Wisdom of the Centuries* (New York: Carol Publishing Group, 1993), 214. Letter to Gerrit Smith, March 30, 1849.
2. Andrew Jackson, cited in *Great Quotes from Great Leaders* (Lombard, IL: Celebrating Excellence Publishing, 1990), 79.
3. Andy Grove, *Only the Paranoid Survive* (New York: Random House, 1999). Grove is the former CEO and current chairman of the board for Intel Corporation.

CHAPTER 3

1. "Diagnosis and Treatment Guidelines on Domestic Violence," *American Medical Association Journal* (1992).

2. S. Plichta, "Violence, Health and Use of Health Service," in *Women's Health and Care Seeking Behavior* (Baltimore: John S. Hopkins University Press).

3. "Abortions in America," *U.S. News & World Report,* January 1999, 20.

4. From the Web site <users.ntr.net1~kenta/roadrage.html>.

5. John McIntosh, "Just the Facts," *American Association of Suicidology,* July 1997.

6. *Citizen's Alert,* a weekly Focus on the Family publication, 22 March 2000.

7. Attorney General's 1986 Commission on Pornography.

8. Dylan Klebold and Eric Harris, the gunmen responsible for the Columbine massacre, also died that day by self-inflicted wounds. Their deaths were not included in the number quoted in this passage.

9. Sandra Sobieraj, "Clinton Wants Violence, Kids Study," *Yahoo! News,* 1 June 1999.

10. Randall Mikkelsen, "Clinton Puts Anti-Violence Spotlight on Hollywood," *Yahoo! News,* 1 June 1999.

11. Leilani Corpus, "Unholy Hollywood," October 1991.

12. Walt Mueller, "Interview with Marilyn Manson," *New Man,* October/November 1998.

CHAPTER 5

1. See the Lord's rebuke to the church in Ephesus (Rev. 2:4), Pergamos (Rev. 2:14–16), Thyatira (Rev. 2:20), Sardis (Rev. 3:1–3), and Laodicea (Rev. 3:15–20).

2. Many scholars conclude that Paul was imprisoned in Rome twice. It is certain that Paul spent two years in Rome under house arrest. According to "Encyclopedia to the Master Study Bible," Paul "had hoped to spend the winter in Nicopolis and while there was probably arrested by some informers and

taken to Rome. This time he was in the Mamertine Dungeon and had no liberty at all." *Master Study Bible* (Nashville: Holman Bible Publishers, 1983), 1690.

3. "According to tradition, the Apocalypse was written in the reign of Domitian" (referring to the writings of Irenaeus, in *Against Heresies* 5.30.3). Cited by Merrill C. Tenney, *New Testament Survey* (Grand Rapids, MI: Eerdmans, 1961), 11–12.

4. If you are a Methodist, Episcopalian, Presbyterian, or Baptist as I was, then you may not be familiar with camp meetings. They are extended worship and preaching meetings attended by saints from many locations. They get their name from the two Great Awakenings (fostered by early Methodist, Baptist, and Presbyterian evangelists in the 1720s to 1740s and 1790s) when people traveled on foot and by horseback for days to hear the Word preached. The only way to accommodate such a crowd was for the people to camp out on the grounds of an open field or campsite.

CHAPTER 6

1. See Matthew 16:13, 15.

2. James Strong, *Strong's Exhaustive Concordance of the Bible* (Peabody, MA: Hendrickson Publishers, n.d.), meanings and definitions drawn from the word derivations for *Jesus* (Greek #2424) and *Yehowshuwa'* (Hebrew #3091), respectively.

3. The name *Oshea* appears twice in the Old Testament, in apparent chronological order. Numbers 13:8 lists "Oshea the son of Nun" as one of the men chosen to spy out the land of Canaan. Numbers 13:16 says Moses called Oshea "Jehoshua," but I believe that reference leaves room to interpret this as occurring after the sortie into Canaan. The first mention of Joshua occurs in Exodus 17:9, when Moses told him to choose some warriors for a battle—well into or toward the end of the forty-year wilderness march.

CHAPTER 7

1. Demerol is a brand-name synthetic narcotic pain reliever and sedative that is often used for the management of long-term chronic pain symptoms.

CHAPTER 8

1. Don't run out and announce that Pastor Rod Parsley says balloons are of the devil, or that fun fairs, clowns, and fun in general have no place in Christian education. My point is simply this: *no one is training our children to learn God's Word today*. All of the fun activities are nothing more than icing on the cake. Our problem is that there is no "cake" under all of that sugar frosting. As for tanning beds, I don't know enough about them to comment one way or the other—unless our motivations for their use cause us to ignore the callings and requirements of God.

2. We will look more closely at the meaning behind the phrase *imposing the kingdom* in the next chapter, "The Violent Take It by Force."

3. James Strong, *Strong's Exhaustive Concordance of the Bible*, meanings and definitions drawn from the extended word applications for the Hebrew word *shuwb* (Hebrew #7725).

CHAPTER 9

1. *Merriam-Webster's Collegiate Dictionary*, 10th ed. (Springfield, MA: Merriam-Webster, 1994), 1003.

2. See Mark 5:8–13, which describes the time Jesus commanded a legion of demons to leave their victim, and they entered a herd of two thousand pigs and destroyed them.

CHAPTER 10

1. Paul wrote in his letter to Titus, "Looking for that *blessed hope*, and the glorious appearing of the great God and our Savior Jesus Christ" (Titus 2:13, italics mine).

2. Read Revelation 21:21: "The twelve gates were twelve pearls; every several gate was of one pearl: and *the street of the city was pure gold,* as it were transparent glass" (italics mine).

CHAPTER 11

1. I spend the rest of the chapter defining what I mean by *travailing prayer.* The word *travail* is used to express what pediatricians, doctors, and mothers around the world mean by the term *labor* in the context of childbirth.

2. Mimi's favorite song was "Will the Circle Be Unbroken?" by A. P. Carter. She incorporated its powerful words into most of her prayers for Willie.

CHAPTER 12

1. According to *Holman's Bible Dictionary,* edited by Trent C. Butler (Nashville: Holman Bible Publishers, 1991), "The early blossom meant for Jeremiah that the almond watched for spring and gave the prophet a wordplay on the almond (Hebrew, *shaqed*) and his task to watch (Hebrew, *shoqed*) (Jer. 1:11)."

CHAPTER 13

1. An *open vision* is a supernatural revelation from God that is received while in a waking state and with the eyes wide open. It is miraculous in nature and relatively rare. I have had only two such visions in my lifetime, and many Christians never receive one. God tends to use open visions to help move us into a position of obedience, to warn of impending danger, or to inspire actions directly related to His purposes.

CHAPTER 14

1. *Strong's Exhaustive Concordance of the Bible,* meanings and definitions drawn from the word derivations for *baqa'* or "divided" (Hebrew #1234).

2. The alternate translations of the words used in this passage are based on the word studies from *Strong's Exhaustive Concordance of the Bible;* meanings and definitions drawn from the word derivations for *fullness* and *time* (Greek #4138 and #5550, respectively).

3. Tamar's story is a complex tale of sin, betrayal, and deception; but suffice it to say she was Judah's daughter-in-law through his son, Er, whom God killed! See Genesis 38 for more details.

4. *Strong's Exhaustive Concordance of the Bible,* meanings and definitions drawn from the word derivations for *Pharez* (Hebrew #6557, #6556, and #6555).

5. Ibid., meanings and definitions drawn from the word derivations for *Mahalaleel* (Hebrew #4111, #410, #352, and #193).

6. Ibid., meanings and definitions for the word *valiant* (Hebrew #2428 and #2342).

ABOUT THE AUTHOR

ROD PARSLEY is pastor of World Harvest Church in Columbus, Ohio, a dynamic megachurch with more than 12,000 in attendance weekly that touches lives worldwide. He is also a highly sought-after crusade and conference speaker who delivers a life-changing message to raise the standard of physical purity, moral integrity, and spiritual intensity. Parsley also hosts *Breakthrough,* a daily and weekly television broadcast seen by millions across America and around the world, as well as oversees Bridge of Hope misssions and outreach, World Harvest Bible College, and World Harvest Academy. He and his wife, Joni, have two children, Ashton and Austin.